THE BBC RADIO SUSSEX GUIDE TO

Peopl
Hidden Sussex

G000138179

by
WARDEN SWINFEN
and
DAVID ARSCOTT

with line drawings by
JOHN WHITING

"Sussex, simple-hearted, loves not her great ones best,
But minds the unwritten multitudes
she bore upon her breast."
(Rev. F. W. Bourdillon)

BBC RADIO SUSSEX

1 MARLBOROUGH PLACE, BRIGHTON

1985

By the same authors:
The BBC Radio Sussex Guide to Hidden Sussex
(Referred to in this book as *Hidden Sussex*)

Note: The sketch map on p.18 is intended merely to give an approximate location. To put 435 names on a map of this size would be impossible, but our sketch will at least indicate where to search on a larger-scale map such as an Ordnance 1/50,000 map or a road atlas.

Front cover: Detail from a print in the 1790 series "Excursion to Brighthelmstone" by Thomas Rowlandson. Kindly made available by Peterson & Short, Print Dealers, Regent Arcade, Brighton.

ISBN 0 9509510 1 3

Photoset and printed in England by Flexiprint Ltd., Lancing, Sussex.

WE ARE ALL, it is said, descended from kings, and so likewise from rogues of the worst sort. The taste of the times seems to favour the latter. Amateur genealogists would once recoil in distaste and fear from evidence of their forefathers' misdemeanours. Today the wayward are more highly prized in this respect than the virtuous, just as humble origins are much preferred (so long as they be humble *enough*). Who would not rather have a highwayman for an ancestor than the bewigged judge who sentenced him; a smuggler than an exciseman; a charcoal burner than the iron-master he served?

Through a similar perverse romanticism the people we most enjoy reading about are, by and large, those with whom we should least relish sharing our day-to-day life. Great eccentrics must make highly uncomfortable flat-sharers; the debauched jags of a Regency buck would find most of us pleading for mercy; while a visit from some of the more colourful ruffians would surely prompt us to hide the kitchen knife. The rôle of these characters, suitably removed in time and space, is to offer our imaginations an escape from the humdrum.

We are tempted, therefore, to warn those 'furriners' among our readers not to interpret our gallery as a true reflection of the Sussex population, past or present. Further thought, however, dissuades us. Certainly we have highlighted the strange and the striking, but in compiling our book we have experienced a growing, kaleidoscopic impression of yesterday's Sussex being recreated in our pages — a random, even chaotic, swarming of trades, professions and callings, the high born and the low, the young and the old, the tragic and the comic, the foolish and the wise. Here artists rub shoulders with murderers, confidence tricksters with prelates, soldiers with dairymaids. The collection is restless with humanity.

Yet our gathering, however rich and various, is not complete. How could it be? Notable residents of the county (and they have been legion) are given a place at table without question, but outsiders have to sing for their supper. Because of its beauty and its proximity to both the capital and the continent, Sussex has always attracted a vast range of holiday-makers and passers-through. Were we to record every instance of a famous person spending a week or two by the sea or taking refreshment at a wayside inn our book would be fat with pointless trivia. In these cases we have looked for the unexpected; for a good story. The less-than-famous present fewer problems: their names have usually come down to us precisely because of some event which is well worth mentioning.

Not that we should expect fair play from the historical record. The secondary rôle of women through the centuries is necessarily reflected in our pages. Similarly, a fascination with the life of Everyman is a recent phenomenon, so that the lower orders all too often appear in unflattering, if diverting, walk-on parts — as prize-fighters, thieves, witches, sufferers from 'the king's evil' and (a considerable smattering of these) cockers of anti-clerical snooks. Then there is the tantalising brevity of many of our early sources. Why did Nicholas de la Beche drag the king out of bed? How did Agnes Devenish come to have the plum stone lodged in her nostril? We shall never know the answers to such questions and had best enjoy these fragments of stories for what they are.

This volume is intended as a companion to *Hidden Sussex* which celebrated the little-known features of some four hundred villages and hamlets. It covers the same rural territory (any one of our larger towns would have demanded a small book of its own) and has an identical format. Once again Warden Swinfen provides a comprehensive introduction; there is a rough sketch map (page 18) with a numbering system to help you at least to set off in the right direction; and we include a short bibliography and an index. The entries are again by villages alphabetically listed, but the names are not exactly the same.

Several places which shyly resisted our investigations the first time around now elbow their way into the throng. Others, having revealed all on that occasion, modestly step back into the shadows. We would ask you to take the two books together: if any settlement of a reasonable size is found to be missing, our pride will be as badly bruised as that of its inhabitants.

The pleasure we take from visiting a place is derived as much from what we bring to it as from what we see. Sometimes (a bare hillside where a battle was fought long ago) our imagination is put to a severe test. At other times (visiting a restored windmill, for example) it may seem that all we need to know stands clear before our eyes. The most memorable occasions, however, are those on which the two components of reality come together — when our prior knowledge gives an extra dimension to the experience of discovery. We hope, therefore, that this second book will be as great a spur to travel the county as our first. (Wear a coat with two large pockets). You will surely find yourself accompanied on your journeys by an invisible host, for these people are still alive in the sense that matters: they have not gone away. Recovering the faint traces of their manifold feats and escapades, we ourselves have come to feel perpetually jostled by a teeming congregation of unquiet, imperishable ghosts.

David Arscott

INTRODUCTION

IN 1865 MARK ANTONY LOWER, doyen of Victorian writers on Sussex history, produced *The Worthies of Sussex*. He collected for it biographical notices of the county's most significant people, from Saint Wilfred to Shelley. And no-one else has done it since — until now.

Not that we have limited ourselves to the Worthies. Sussex notables have ever comprised the tops and the bottoms, while those in the middle have tended to be more ordinary, more orderly — though this is not, we suppose, a characteristic of Sussex alone. 120 years ago, in Lower's day, more stress was laid than nowadays upon the virtues of respectability and benevolence; though even then he felt unable to omit the rebel Jack Cade.

As with our previous volume, *Hidden Sussex*, we have left out the major towns. Our largest 'villages' (a generic term covering all smaller communities and not to be exactly defined) are probably Midhurst, Crowborough and Hailsham, and no place is too small if we could find a candidate. We have once again driven hundreds of miles in our quest. The vivid personalities we have found have often hitherto gone unsung, and have been located only by persistent inquiry. We have chatted to local residents, we have deciphered tombstones and monuments, we have scanned walls, doors and floors alike. We have not neglected the standard books on our county, as witness our list for further reading, but we have been probing ever deeper in an effort to bring between our covers the more out-of-the-way, forgotten, material. The need for selectivity has often been forced upon us, as over the centuries some villages have been the home of too many denizens of distinction. We have tried not to tell the same story twice — you will search these pages in vain for Grey Owl and Jim Pulk, since they figured in *Hidden Sussex*. But to help frustrated researchers we have often inserted a back-reference.

Our guidelines have directed us towards the infamous rather than the famous where space was rationed, so many of the divines whom Lower deemed Worthies have no place here. No doubt they were, extremely, worthy, but to us they often seemed earnest, dry and colourless — and colourful characters are much more fun to read about, as David Arscott has

4

made clear. Yet to attempt such a book as this and to omit all mention of Cardinal Manning or the Frewen family, among others, would be downright purblind, so they have their niches.

The problem of the great families is a grave one, which could only be fully solved by devoting to them a whole book. The de Braoses in Norman times, the Tudor Howards, the Pelhams and the de la Warrs, for example, all demand coverage. Perhaps this is best given in an Introduction not tied to any particular village name. Since lineage is rarely traceable back to Saxon times, we must begin at 1066, the most fateful year for Sussex — not because of the great battle so much as because many of the conquering army stayed and settled here, moulding its people and its history.

The five 'rapes' of Sussex were allotted by Norman William as follows: Hastings to the Count of Eu; Pevensey to Count Robert of Mortain or Morton, half-brother to the Conqueror himself; Lewes to William de Warenne; Bramber to William de Braose or Briouze; and Arundel to Roger de Montgomeri. The sixth rape, Chichester, was formed only in the thirteenth century by the division of Arundel Rape, which was twice the size of the others anyway. But not all of them remained for long in their families; the honours of Earls Robert and Roger were forfeited by their respective sons. Ownership does not imply personal occupation, as most of the land was let out to occupant farmers. The system was too involved to discuss here, but full details are in the Victoria County History of Sussex, Vol. 1, p.377 and on.

Robert, Count of Eu, was rewarded by William the Conqueror around 1069 with the honour and barony of Hastings, but not for his feats on Senlac field. The royal security was threatened in several directions, and Count Robert had been dispatched to Lincolnshire to combat a strong Danish invasion. He defeated them so soundly that such a reward was only his due. William had, too, deeper motives of policy; Count Robert owned large areas of land across the Channel, so by this means the sea passage between Normandy and Hastings could be placed in safe hands. On Robert's death, about 1090, his son William supported the king's opponents. He was arrested for conspiracy in 1095, condemned to be blinded, and died soon afterwards. Succeeding generations took sides either for or against the monarch of the time, making them appear a thoroughly quarrelsome family. When in 1186 Count Raoul died a minor, the estate passed to his sister Alice, who married Ralph de Lusignan. King John in 1201 picked a quarrel with de Lusignan and seized the entire Rape of Hastings, bestowing it on Alice's uncle John de Eu, who was loyal. John de Eu died in 1207, whereupon King John took the lands back for himself, only to return them a few years later to Ralph and Alice. Ralph died in 1219 leaving Alice in sole possession. In 1225 Henry III forced her to surrender her lands to him, because she was French and Henry was then at war with France. Despite several promises, the Eu family never recovered their Sussex possessions.

Robert of Mortain built a castle at Pevensey, inside the walls of the old Roman castle. Hither came his brother Odo of Bayeux, who had been a supporter of William Rufus's elder brother Robert, deprived by William of his rightful heritage of the throne. The castle was besieged and eventually taken. The King confiscated Count Robert's estates as punishment for sheltering the rebellious Odo, and the Mortain family fades from Sussex history. The same thing happened to Arundel in the next reign — Henry I — when Robert, son of Roger de Montgomeri, rebelled unsuccessfully in 1101 and was banished, his lands being forfeit to the king.

The de Warennes had links through marriage with the Norman royal family. William the Conqueror's daughter Gundrada was the wife of William de Warenne, who fought at the battle of Hastings. Afterwards, the Conqueror gave to de Warenne vast tracts of land in Norfolk, Surrey and other counties, together with the town and the entire Rape of Lewes as his domain. Having regard to its elevated position and its accessibility by river, de Warenne decided to make Lewes his chief residence. He speedily began the construction of a splendid castle on what was probably already a fortified site. Then, about 1075, he and his wife set forth on pilgrimage to Rome. On their way they rested at the great abbey of Cluny, and were so impressed by it and the monks of the order that they resolved to bring the Cluniac ideal to England. On returning home they founded the Priory of St Pancras at Southover, in 1077, liberally endowing it with churches and manors — Ardingly, Clayton, Cuckfield, Ditchling and many more. Among the ancient stained glass in Ardingly church is a shield "chequy or and azure" (i.e., a chessboard pattern of gold and blue squares) — the de Warenne arms.

Neither Gundrada nor William saw their priory complete. They were buried in small leaden coffins in the hallowed grounds, where they rested until 1845. Then workmen digging the railway line through the neglected ruins unexpectedly came across the two ancient coffins. They were reverently removed and re-interred in Southover church, where they still lie.

Their successors were made Earls of Warenne and Surrey; in 1312 King Edward II granted his friend John de Warenne, Earl of Surrey, a charter to hold an annual fair at Ditchling. This was in those days not an uncommon way for royalty to show its generosity, as several entries in our pages will show. (However, Royalty could also unmake its generous acts — at the Dissolution of the Monasteries in the 1530s Henry VIII gave Ditchling Manor to Thomas Cromwell, but he was disgraced in 1541, so Henry took it back and gave it to

Anne of Cleves instead.) The eighth earl of the line died in 1347 and title passed to his sister Alice. She was the wife of Edmund Fitz-Alan, Earl of Arundel, whose heirs now are the Dukes of Norfolk and the Earls of Abergavenny and de la Warr.

William de Braose was chancellor to, and almost certainly a kinsman of, the Conqueror, and for his loyal support was rewarded with no fewer than forty-one Sussex manors, besides many more in other counties. By 1073 he had built Bramber castle and founded a borough (which prospered little) beside it.

He built a causeway and bridge over the river Arun and charged a toll for its use. He also founded a collegiate church, which became the subject of repeated disputes with Fécamp abbey in Normandy, who owned nearby Steyning. It was dissolved somewhere around 1090, the endowment being transferred to a new priory, Sele, at Upper Beeding (see *Hidden Sussex*). William died about 1095, his son Philip succeeding him. The date of Philip's death is unknown, but his son, another William, was certainly in possession between 1155 and 1192. William's son, the third William, lost his lands around 1208 or perhaps 1212, through confiscation by King John, who put to death his wife and his four youngest children. However, the family recovered them in 1226. The last William de Braose in 1316 settled the lordship of Bramber on John, Lord Mowbray, and his wife Aline, one of William's daughters and heirs, and the direct de Braose line came to an end. The name occurs in parish records from Shipley in the north to Southwick in the south, often in connection with the building of churches. For instance, a decree of 1103 declared that the de Braoses were to hold the tenements of Steyning borough; and one of the Williams died in the manor house at Findon in 1290. By another line, incidentally, the de Braoses were ancestors of several kings of Scotland — Braose apparently becoming modified to Bruce.

The complex ramifications of the Fitz-Alan and Howard families can most easily be explained by outlining the story from the time of Henry I. The forfeiture of the Arundel estates to the Crown upon the treason of William de Montgomeri was mentioned above. Henry I settled them on his queen Adeliza, who outlived her royal husband by many years. Soon after the king's death in 1135 she married William de Albini who thus acquired the title Earl of Arundel. Under the French spelling of his name, D'Aubigny, he is recorded as co-founder with Robert de la Haye (founder of the Benedictine abbey at Lessay) of Boxgrove Priory. As part of the endowment of the priory he gave to it, among other properties, Barnham church (1105). The fifth earl, Hugh de Albini, died childless in 1243 and the title passed through his sister Isabel to her husband John Fitzalan, lord of Clun and Oswaldestre in Shropshire. The Fitzalan family thus acquired Arundel castle and held it and the title with great distinction. Ultimately Henry Fitzalan, the 14th and last Earl of Arundel, sought the hand in marriage of no less a person than Queen Elizabeth I. Being rejected, he became something of a recluse, dying in 1580. His only son, Lord Maltravers, and his elder daughter both predeceased him, so the family estate passed to the younger daughter Mary. While still a mere child she had been married to Thomas Howard, fourth Duke of Norfolk, the unlucky man whose aspiration to the hand of Mary Queen of Scots caused a furious Queen Elizabeth to have him beheaded. The Duke by the laws of those times came into possession of the castle, lands and honours which his descendants still hold today, despite forfeitures later reversed and similar interruptions. But it was not this marriage that brought the honour of Earl Marshal of England into the Norfolk family: that had come earlier, through the lines of Mowbray and Thomas Plantagenet back in the latter part of the 13th century.

The Dalyngridges spelt their name in many different ways, but it remains readily recognisable. They come into the Sussex story round about 1370, and although their closest connection is with Bodiam they can be traced in Robertsbridge, Penhurst, Bramber and elsewhere. Indeed, they may well have started in East Grinstead. Bodiam castle and manor, prior to about 1367, had belonged to a family named Wardedieux or Wardeux; but around that time Elizabeth, daughter and heiress of John de Wardeux, married Sir Edward Dalyngrigge and brought him Bodiam as her dowry. Born in 1346, he had achieved a position of trust and eminence under King Richard II, who gave him several Sussex estates. In 1392 he was made Keeper of the Tower of London and Governor of the City, but he died some three years later. He was granted a licence to crenellate Bodiam castle in 1386 and took the opportunity for a complete rebuild, creating the romantic and beautiful building whose ruins we see today. Sir Edward was not only powerful but ruthless, keeping a gang of roughs to police his estates. He engaged in frequent skirmishes with the officers of John of Gaunt, Duke of Lancaster, whose father, King Edward III, had given him hunting rights in Ashdown Forest. Dalyngrigge considered himself paramount lord in those parts and set his mob to drive Lancaster out. The Duke tried to buy Sir Edward off by appointing him master forester of Ashdown; but the plan misfired, as Dalyngrigge would brook no interference with his freedom to do exactly as he liked. Dalyngrigge was soon dismissed from the forester's office, but he was too powerful in the area to be brought to justice, even when in 1384 some of his henchmen murdered a sub-forester.

Sir Edward's son, Sir John Dalyngrigge, was childless, so that eventually the estate passed to his first cousin Philippa. She married twice, her second husband being Sir Thomas Lewknor, Kt., of a long-established Sussex family. The Dalyngrigges by the fourteenth century had become well dispersed. There is in Fletching church a brass to a member of the family; precisely which one is uncertain, but probably Sir Walter (died c. 1380) and his wife.

8

John of Gaunt's main link with Sussex comes through his love of hunting. He had hunting lodges at several places including Ashurstwood and Pevensey. He surrendered his title of Earl of Richmond to his father Edward III in exchange for the honour of Pevensey. But he left a permanent memorial of a different kind — his crest, a white hart, has furnished a name for many "locals" in our area.

The name Lewknor crops up well away from Bodiam, at Kingston Buci and even Trotton in the fifteenth century. Tracing the family history is not made easier by the repetition in each generation of the christian names Roger and Thomas. Philippa, mentioned above, was the mother of Sir Roger Lewknor of Dedisham, who in turn had two sons, inevitably Thomas and Roger. Sir Thomas (of Trotton) was born c. 1456 and owned Bodiam for much of his life. He adhered to the Lancastrian cause during the Wars of the Roses, and when Richard III came to the throne paid the penalty of attainder for treason. He retreated into the fastnesses of Bodiam, which the king ordered should be besieged by a force headed by Sir Thomas's own uncle, Richard Lewknor of Brambletye — this was in 1483. The castle soon surrendered, Sir Thomas being disgraced as a rebel. However, after King Richard's defeat and death at Bosworth in 1485, he was reinstated. His son, another Sir Roger, who was Sheriff of Sussex in 1532, married three times without having the fortune of a son and heir. He had, though, at least five daughters, all of whom married and took portions of the Bodiam estates as dowries to their husbands. In consequence, this branch of the Lewknors ceased to bear the family name after influencing the history of the county for over four centuries. The name was not extinct, however, as other branches lived in various parts of West Sussex. One Sir John Lewknor, lord of the manor of Goring, was slain at the battle of Tewkesbury in 1471 and the manor was escheated to the Crown. We note a much later Christopher Lewknor under *West Dean (West Sussex).*

The Nevill family is another with long associations in Sussex. Their founder, Gilbert de Nevill, is said to have been William the Conqueror's admiral. However, the Sussex estates were acquired through the female line. The well-known Abergavenny title was originally Burgavenny, and belonged to the Beauchamp family. In the early fourteenth century the then Lord Burgavenny was created Earl of Worcester by Henry V after Agincourt. His daughter and heiress, Lady Elizabeth Beauchamp, married Sir Edward Nevill and brought to him not only the Burgavenny title and estates but also those of the Despencers. Sir Edward, who was the uncle of two kings, Edward IV and Richard III, became Lord Burgavenny and as such was summoned to Parliament in 1450 by Henry VI. His wife held several manors in Sussex — she is recorded as owning Rodmell in 1439. It says much for family tenacity that the freehold of Rodmell manor was sold by the then Lord Abergavenny as recently as 1919.

At the time of Edward's death in 1476 the family seat was at Eridge Castle, but they gradually deserted it in favour of Kidbrooke, near East Grinstead. During the earlier times at Eridge, one of the Burgavennys was Henry Nevill, a favourite of Queen Elizabeth I. She spent several days at the Castle during her "progress" through Kent and Sussex in 1573. The old title was changed to Abergavenny in 1724, in which year William, the then Earl, began the building of the present Kidbrooke mansion. It was well in use by 1736, as this date appears in several places in the house. In 1743 an Act of Settlement was passed in William's favour, but he died the next year: he is buried in East Grinstead church. Henry, the second Earl, decided to return to Eridge and an extraordinary mansion was built for him in 1787 by an amateur architect who gave it a period flavour by having medieval trimmings dabbed on all over it. (Unhappily, the bulk of the old castle was demolished just before World War II.) The family has continued to reside in Sussex until the present day, and to give its name to several local pubs. In our own day Lord Rupert Nevill, a cousin of the Queen, lives at Little Horsted and from time to time has the honour of entertaining members of the Royal Family.

In 1511 George Nevill, Lord Burgavenny, enfranchised Andrew Borde, a remarkable man in many ways. His brother Richard held the manors of Northeye, Pevensey and Westham in East Sussex, but although Andrew did for a time live in Pevensey, his better-known connections are around Cuckfield. He was born at Borde's Hill in Holmesdale near Cuckfield and graduated as a 'doctor of physick' at Montpelier and Oxford Universities. He was for a time a favourite at the court of Henry VIII, to whom he was court physician. But he was a restless soul and spent much of his life travelling as a quack doctor with country fairs. His bubbly personality earned him the nickname 'Merry Andrew' — and the phrase has passed into the English language. For a while he lived as a Carthusian friar but found the life too severe, though he was a respected theologian and astrologer. He wrote a number of books on health and travel, well larded with philosophical ruminations. Later in life he enjoyed travel, and even became a political spy. He ended his days in 1549, a debtor in the Fleet prison in London.

The de la Warr title is of more recent foundation. The Sussex connection rests initially upon Thomas West, second holder of the title, who owned Halnaker House and was patron of the church at Boxgrove. He wished to be buried here with his wife Elizabeth, and built in the church a chantry chapel where masses were to be said for the repose of their souls. The chantry, begun in 1532, was never completed, for the Dissolution was only a few years away. The priory of Boxgrove was suppressed and the chantry narrowly escaped destruction. It was saved by Lord de la Warr, who first appealed for "his power chapell to be buryed in" and, when that failed, bought the priory from the king. Shortly afterwards he left the neighbourhood and was eventually buried at Broadwater. At least, so one gathers from the history books; but the date on the tomb is 1526, so maybe that was the date of the first earl's death, since the Boxgrove chapel clearly carries the date 1532. The earl set up on the walls and ceiling of the chapel the arms of all the owners of Halnaker, so that it becomes a potted history of the mansion. The site of Boxgrove Priory at the Dissolution was granted to Thomas de la Warr for the sum of £126. 13s. 4d.

The story of the Pelham family is one whose opening chapters are obscure. They are first recorded in the mid-fourteenth century when they were tenants of John de Vere, Earl of Oxford, at Laughton. They rose in the world and soon became lords of the manor of Laughton. The famous story of the Pelham buckle (see *Halland* in *Hidden Sussex*) dates from the battle of Poitiers in 1356. During the same period branches of the family spread over the county; one Sir John Pelham bought the manor of River, near Petworth, in 1399 and his descendants held it for nearly a century. In 1425 a Sir John Pelham — perhaps the same one — obtained possession of his manor at Crowhurst, at the other end of the county, on the expiry of a lease. This branch of the family has continued to hold it right into the twentieth century, although owing to at least one instance of a female heir (Anne Pelham, who married Col. Thomas Papillon in the early nineteenth century), the surname Pelham as lord of the manor has become extinct.

The principal family home was at Laughton Place, which was then moated and fortified. A lofty tower dated 1534 was built to command a wide view of the countryside. Although Laughton Place is now a farmhouse, the landmark tower still proudly stands. A couple of years earlier, in 1532, William Pelham had been a courtier in attendance on King Henry VIII at the Field of Cloth of Gold. In 1591 Sir Thomas Pelham acquired the entire castle, rape and lordship of Hastings. He was created a baronet in 1611, and in 1706 another Sir Thomas, his great-great-grandson, was ennobled as Baron Pelham of Laughton. His son inherited the title six years later, and in 1715 he was created Duke of Newcastle. This Pelham — another Thomas — lived on until 1768, but as he was childless the succession went to a cousin, Thomas Pelham of Stanmer, who was created Earl of Chichester in 1801. The earldom of Chichester has remained in the family to the present time. Although the family built another house in 1595 at nearby Halland — which no longer exists — Laughton retained their loyalty. In the Pelham vault of Laughton church, sealed in 1866 after the interment of the third Earl, lie more than thirty coffins, including those of two Prime Ministers, a bishop of Lincoln, one Duke of Newcastle and three Earls of Chichester.

Upon the death of Queen Elizabeth I and the accession of the Stuart line, a profound change came over England. The whole pattern of life seems to alter, and our attention is drawn from the great families to humbler folk. Some trades there always have been — mills were recorded in Domesday — but new industry was flourishing in Sussex. There seems to have been a group of Flemish emigré glassworkers around Kirdford in the fourteenth century, but their output must be classed as craftsmanship rather than industry. Iron was another matter. Iron had been found here by the fifteenth century, and for several hundred years cannon, farm tools and firebacks were among the products of a true industry. Ralph Hogge of Buxted is said to have made the first English cast-iron cannon in 1543, and the last furnace, at Ashburnham, finally closed almost 300 years later. In some places the defunct iron workings were replaced by gunpowder manufacture, sometimes with disastrous consequences (see *Brede, Sedlescombe*). Ironworking is nowadays considered a heavy industry, but the women of Sussex had enough of both skill and strength to take part; see *Northchapel* and *Netherfield*. We are dubious about Jhone Colens, mentioned under Burwash in *Hidden Sussex*; because to us Jhone sounds like Joan, "she" has been claimed as an ironmistress. But we think the name is just John with the silent final E of Olde Dayes. All the same, widows of hard-working Sussex men often did continue their husbands' trades, be they ironmasters, millers, blacksmiths or whatever.

The insatiable furnaces consumed huge quantities of fuel provided by the dense Sussex forests. Wood not used in this way went sometimes for building ships, more often for building houses, so that vast tracts of the Wealden 'forests' are now open heaths, with gorse, bracken and low scrub. Nevertheless, the void left by the wholesale felling of trees conjures up its own image of Sussex folk, bronzed and brawny, pursuing active occupations which have left their own memorials. It is almost impossible to drive more than a few miles along a Sussex by-road without finding a timber-framed house or cottage. Many are still lived in and loved by modern folk for whom the old ways are worth conserving. Most have frames filled with wattle and daub — a most instructive example is the Priest House at West Hoathly, now a delightful museum. Our observations lead us to think that the overhanging upper storey, or 'jetty', is not a conspicuous Sussex feature. This is not to say that none can be found, but that a walk through an old town or village like Rye or Midhurst will reveal as many house fronts flat as jettied. The reason may lie in the dependable Sussex oak, or may be in many instances the lower floor wall was built flush with the jetty.

Over the years prosperity rewarded those who worked hard on their lands. With prosperity farm labourers became farmers, farmers became yeomen, and so on up the scale. As standards improved, so did the desire for security and comfort. Wattle and daub began to be replaced by the safer and more durable brick, locally made, thanks to the heavy Wealden clay which proved ideal for brickmaking. At its peak this thriving industry could boast of kilns every few miles, traces of many of which can still be found. The best clay, however, was in the north of the county, where Warnham and Southwater have long been centres of brick production. Useful supplies of lime and chalk were waiting to be tapped along the line of the South Downs. The great workings near Amberley, long disused, have been turned into an exciting museum appropriately called 'Chalkpits', but the gigantic cement works at the back of Shoreham is still very active. Further inland, around Petworth in particular, dense deposits of the fossil remains of a small snail, *Paludina fluviorum*, have coalesced to form a beautiful blue-grey stone generally (though inaccurately) called 'Sussex marble'. It is easily carved and polished, so that our ancestors have left us noble examples of their art in gravestones, fonts and furnishing of all kinds, in both churches and houses.

Other tradesmen remained at least partly itinerant, especially if their products were not in continuous demand. Bryan Eldridge and John Waylett were both travelling bell-founders, and another founder, William Hull, was working at Malling in the late seventeenth century. Eldridge was head of the great foundry at Chertsey in Surrey; before him, Richard Eldridge, probably his father, had a foundry in Horsham until 1622. Bryan Eldridge's bells still hang in many Sussex churches, including Kirdford (two, dated 1642 and 1649), Climping (1636 and 1654) and Beddingham (1639). The third bell at St. Nicholas, Portslade, was by Bryan and William Eldridge and is dated 1661 — the year of Bryan's death. William was probably his son, because a bell by William in Boxgrove Priory is dated 1674, and there are later ones. John Waylett was working in the early eighteenth century; he worked very much "on the spot", casting his bells right in the churchyard or by the nearest hammerpond. Three of his bells hang in Laughton church tower, and another is at Mayfield — all dated 1724 or 1725. Some three dozen bells of his are known in Sussex belfries.

However, the great majority of Sussex workers were engaged on the land. The shepherd's life may have been lonely, but it seems to have bred great strength of character and a gift for original philosophy, as our index entry 'Shepherds' shows. Tools were essential for the job, and Pyecombe is still remembered as the great centre for making crooks; a crook is worked into the roadside signs for the village. Side by side with crooks went the making of bells for sheep and cattle. Several museums have good collections of such bells; Horsham, Worthing and Wilmington Priory are only three. Hove has a set of tuned oxbells from the vanished village of Exceat, and Henfield museum has eight tuned crooks, charmingly musical but puzzlingly unpractical. The other requirement for the shepherd was a supply of hurdles, made locally in the Sussex woodland. Hazel was the favourite wood and the working of it into lengths for fencing, wattles for sheep-pens, or conical feeding cages was a skilled craft in which deftness counted for more than brute strength. Different varieties of hazel were best suited to different soils; the white hazel was best on clay, the darker variety easier to work if grown on chalk. The woodman usually worked on the ground where the trees grew in a clearing. After fulfilling immediate local orders, he would move on a few miles to the next.

Sussex folk have always been known for a sturdy, even mulish, independence of spirit. Under our index entry 'Church, behaviour in' we direct the reader to a few choice specimens. They had — as they still have — strong ideas of what was right and wrong. Official complaints often took the form of a "presentation" to the parish or hundred council; not a bit like its modern counterpart. The records contain hundreds of examples of reports beginning with the words "We present ..." (*e.g. Boxgrove, Coldwaltham*). The process must have been akin to a reprimand.

Of political stubbornness our earliest example must surely be that of Jack Cade, whose rebellion of 1450 is remembered at *Cade Street*. Our most recent is that of Richard Cobden of *Heyshott*, leader of a small group of determined opponents of the iniquitous Corn Laws whose repeal in 1846 constitutes his eternal monument. In between came the Civil War mentioned later on, and the troubles brought about by the Industrial Revolution and the collapse of so much cottage industry. In the 1830s the "Swing Riots" (see *Frant*, and *East Preston* in *Hidden Sussex*) caused more local unrest than any uprising since Cade's.

But sturdy independence takes many forms, political, religious or otherwise. In the mid-sixteenth century successive changes of church doctrine and allegiance under Henry VIII, Mary and Elizabeth I inevitably provoked opposition. Complaints about the restoration of Catholicism under Mary caused the protesters to be anathematized as heretics, and strong action was taken against them. In April 1555 a man of Withyham was ordered to be arrested for seditious preaching. Two months later it was decreed that Derrick Carver, a Brighton brewer, and two other heretics, should be burned — a decree which was speedily executed. In 1556 a total of some thirteen people, men and women, suffered a similar fate in various Sussex towns. In June 1557 the persecution reached its climax with the burning in Lewes market place of five men and five women. The 'Lewes Martyrs', as they have come to be known, included a prominent ironmaster from Warbleton, Richard Woodman. In all some 36 names of Protestant martyrs from Sussex are known to us.

When after the advent of Elizabeth I the tables were turned, a long period of persecution of the Catholics ensued. In Sussex the 'recusant' families, who

14

continued to adhere to the Roman church, included the Gages of Firle and Bentley, the Shelleys of Warminghurst and Michelgrove, the Carylls, Copleys and Lewknors. However, in this period only three people of Sussex actually died for their faith: Edward Shelley (executed at Tyburn, August 1588) and two priests (arrested at Littlehampton and executed on the Broyle Heath later the same year).

The Civil War of the mid-seventeenth century, and the rivalries between Cavaliers and Roundheads, made a great impact on Sussex. The story of the flight through the county of the future King Charles II in 1651, and of his hairsbreadth escapes from capture, is often told, but we cannot avoid occasionally retelling parts of it. Repeatedly in our pages you will read of Royalists, generally aristocratic, who suffered from too overt a display of their sympathies. Sussex was not a predominantly Royalist county. Chichester in particular was held by the Roundhead faction for some while before the close of the Civil War. The head of the Parliamentary party inside the city walls was William Cawley, a local resident who was able to organize resistance to a siege despite a Royalist advance to West Dean, only a few miles away. The Puritans had a penchant for inflicting unlovely, if moral, christian names on their children, and we have captured a number of these (see *Puritans* in subject index).

Notwithstanding the great events and movements of the past, the great virtue of Sussex has been its modesty. Perhaps moderation in the landscape has borne results on the county character. No rugged mountain peaks, no vast sheets of open water, no surging river torrents have wrought their influence on the people whose home has been here, be they native or immigrant. The works of man have been likewise unassuming. Not for Sussex are the soaring wool churches of East Anglia. We have no abbey ruins to compare with Fountains or Tintern, no stately homes to name alongside Blenheim or Castle Howard. Our churches are humble, our castles homely, our houses snug. Down the arcade of the centuries Sussex folk have been dogged, unpretentious — and content. The charm of intimacy has proved a spur to the works of peace. Sussex has offered a home to uncounted artists, writers and thinkers, and it is worthy of note how many of these have allowed the county atmosphere to cast its spell. Several of our greatest writers — Hudson, Jefferies — were naturalists; others — Shelley, Blake — infinitely receptive to the subtle magic of countryside and coast. The music of Edward Elgar and John Ireland, among others, during their time in Sussex is overlaid with a kind of autumnal glow for whose beauty Sussex may take credit. Yet (and Shelley is the glorious exception) these geniuses have been mostly immigrant. Our homebred talents have been minor, and perhaps this too is the result of geography. Thomas Otway, Charlotte Smith and James Hurdis are hardly among the all-time greats of English literature. But they are not forgotten — and perhaps they, too, are content.

However, the people whose achievements set them above the common run of folk are merely the veneer over the basic durable timber of the workaday. Most homes were occupied by the farmers, the millers, the blacksmiths and so on — and the smugglers. Smuggling was in the eighteenth century a well-organised, even respectable, industry in which the law and the church might often gang up against the hated excisemen. The best joke was played by one Nick Cossum, well-known for handling contraband. One day he was walking along a road with a tub of gin when an exciseman stopped him and demanded his tub. Nick meekly surrendered it and said, "However, I'm a-goin' your road and we can talk together — there ain't no law against that." So the exciseman took the tub on his shoulders and the two walked along chatting until they came to a crossroads, where Nick wished the exciseman goodbye. He walked off for some yards, then turned back and said, "Oh, there's one thing I forgot; here's a little bit o' paper that belongs to the keg." "Why, that's a permit", said the exciseman. "Why didn't you show it to me when I took the tub?" "Why", said Nick, "If I'd a-done that you wouldn't have carried my tub for me all this way, would you?"

Of eccentrics, too, Sussex has a full share. Jack Fuller of Brightling, Baron Erskine of Pease Pottage and John Olliver the miller of Highdown are among our more colourful characters; but we warmed to the story of Master Coombs, a miller near Newhaven, who used to paint his mill-horse in different colours, so that he would go to market one week on a yellow mount, next week on a green or blue one — reminiscent of *The Wizard of Oz*. He once uttered some (undisclosed) statement as a fact, and vowed that if it were not so he would never enter his mill again. The statement was shown to be untrue, and he kept his word. He thereafter spent hours each day on the top step of the stairs to the mill door but never again went inside.

The next profound change to come upon our county dates from the years around 1800, and is almost entirely due to improvements in transport. In the 1750s Dr. John Burton had cause to complain of the appalling state of the roads when he visited his mother at Shermanbury, but whatever else the splenetic William Cobbett found to protest about seventy years later, on his *Rural Rides*, bad transport was not commonly his butt. Roads, though, were not the only means of transport. During the quarter century starting in 1790 there was a great surge of canal building, partly for military defence but mainly for agricultural improvement, since they provided a cheap means of moving heavy farm produce and requisites. The earlier canals were dug to improve the usefulness of rivers for transport, so they are strictly classed as 'navigations'. Of canals proper, with locks, the chief examples in Sussex are the Arun-Wey and the Chichester-Arun canals. Their construction provided much local employment, and when finished they were for a while a great boon to farmers. They were killed off by the arrival of the railways.

The expansion of London as the world centre of commerce made it increasingly an unattractive place to live in. Thanks to the ease of access afforded by the tarmacadaming of roads and the reliability of the train, living in one of half-a-dozen counties and going to London each day became a possible, even attractive, way of life. Sussex had the supreme advantage of the warmth of the Channel shore, so that at the end of each rail or road line the growth of residential areas reached epidemic proportions. By the 1930s more people in the county were engaged in the hotel and catering industries than in any other form of work. Half a century later a new balance is emerging. During the last two decades wine has become an important Sussex product. If cinemas close and the minstrels no longer perform on the pier, residents and visitors in their thousands flock to castles and stately homes. The county boasts more than a hundred museums, and it has become almost the rule that if you open the door of an ancient church in summertime you will find someone else inside. So, although the pattern has changed and is changing, the exuberant vitality which is reflected in our pages still emerges as the outstanding quality of the People of Hidden Sussex.

Warden Swinfen
August 1985.

Belle Tout lighthouse

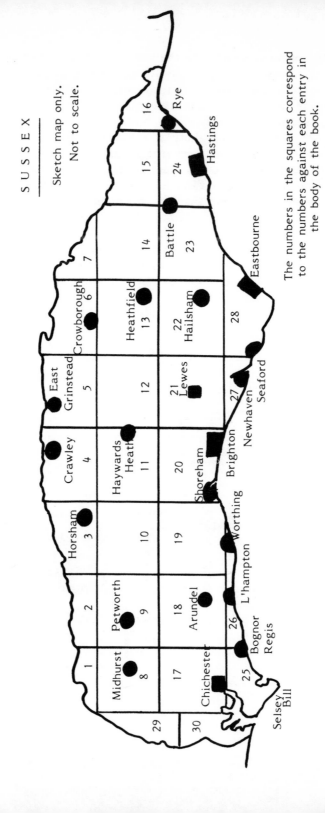

S U S S E X

Sketch map only.
Not to scale.

The numbers in the squares correspond
to the numbers against each entry in
the body of the book.

16

Rye

15

24

Hastings

14

Battle

23

Eastbourne

7

Crowborough

6

Heathfield

13

22

Hailsham

28

East
Grinstead

5

12

21

Lewes

27

Seaford

Newhaven

Crawley

4

Haywards
Heath

11

20

Shoreham

Brighton

Horsham

3

10

19

Worthing

L'hampton

Petworth

2

9

18

Arundel

26

Bognor
Regis

Midhurst

1

8

17

Chichester

25

Selsey
Bill

29

30

18

ADVERSANE

'I have done trimming cows and goats feet, mending the childrens toys and hoops, their prams. Putting ferrules on their walking sticks. I have put a ferrule on a wooden leg for a man on two occasions.'

The memoirs of the village blacksmith Gaius Carley ('Written by Himself' as the title-page proudly claims) were published in 1963. They'd never win a prize for literature but they offer a glimpse of a life that has gone. Gaius worked in several villages before settling in Adversane and, apart from tales of the smithies, we read about hop-picking, bird-scaring and how he wrote love letters for an illiterate gipsy. He also wrote some creaking but robust verses under the title 'The Song of the Blacksmith':

> *Nearly sixty years work in the jolly old forge*
> *Sometimes pleasant, sometimes rough,*
> *Trying to please horses and horsemen,*
> *It's made me jolly well tough.* [10]

ALBOURNE

The man who kept the secret of King Charles I's last words lived at Albourne Place. He was William Juxon, later Archbishop of Canterbury. As the Bishop of London he attended the king on the scaffold and was imprisoned by Cromwell for refusing to give details of their conversation. He was deprived of his bishopric but at the Restoration was created Archbishop, and — the wheel coming full circle — he crowned Charles II king. Local legend has it that he was responsible for an extra large chimney at Albourne Place. Hunted by Cromwell's men, he's said to have disguised himself as a bricklayer, adding to the structure all the time that they were in the grounds looking for him!

Although the Cooperative movement is commonly thought to have begun with the Rochdale Pioneers in 1844, Dr William King actually beat them to it in Brighton by nearly 20 years with a venture that spread to Albourne. Dr King, who settled in Brighton after marrying the daughter of the Vicar of Rottingdean, gave his services to people who couldn't afford to pay and was involved with various educational projects including the local Mechanics Institute, where he taught mathematics. When this folded up in 1827 some of his pupils formed the Cooperative Trading Association — raising capital by weekly contributions to enable members to start trading among themselves. Land was acquired at Albourne and farmed by the association, which finally stopped trading in 1830.

We mentioned the Victorian inventor James Starley in *Hidden Sussex*. He was responsible for the Social Tricycle, which accommodated courting couples side by side. Harry Dacre wrote the music hall song about it:

> *....you'll look sweet*
> *upon the seat*
> *of a bicycle made for two.* [20]

ALCISTON

In the Middle Ages the manor was held by the monks of Battle Abbey, who were once described as 'considerate and painstaking landlords'. Just before the Dissolution of the Monasteries it was granted to Sir William Gage. In the 1930s there lived here (when she was not lecturing at University) Professor Caroline Spurgeon, an authority on English literature and especially on William Blake (see *Felpham*). Besides many articles and essays, she wrote a penetrating analysis of Mysticism in English Poetry.
[22]

ALDINGBOURNE

Nothelm, king of the South Saxons, gave land here in 692 AD for a church and 'monastry' at the request of his sister Nothgitha. Here, too, was a palace of the bishops of Selsey before the see was transferred to Chichester. The present Mill Pond was once the clergy fishpond. Later the palace was extended by the bishops of Chichester, until it was at last seized and destroyed during the Civil War by Parliamentary troops under Sir William Waller.

A modern window in the south wall of the church is in memory of Sir Reginald Skelton, a naval engineer who accompanied Scott on his first voyage to the Antarctic. He eventually became an Engineer Admiral. The choir stalls are in memory of Lady Skelton and Admiral Sir Reginald Henderson.   [17]

ALDRINGTON

It was in 1402 that Thomas (or William) Bolle, rector of the parish, wanted to stop his world and get off. He petitioned the bishop of Chichester for a licence to build a hermit cell by the side of Aldrington church, in which to pass the rest of his life in solitude, prayer and meditation. He specifically undertook to pray for the honour and glory of the Trinity, the Virgin Mary, St. Richard of Chichester and all other saints — perhaps a good way of ingratiating himself and securing his wishes! His petition was granted, and apparently he was duly immured.

In 1724 the parsonage was the only remaining house in the parish, and in 1860 the living was a complete sinecure. When a fresh incumbent was appointed, he went through the ceremony of reading-in (full morning and evening services and other rites), mounted on the pile of stones which was all that remained of the old church. The ceremony used to attract considerable numbers of sightseers.   [20]

ALDSWORTH

We tell of the building of Racton tower by the Earl of Halifax in *Hidden Sussex*. Halifax was born in 1716 and in 1741 married Ann Dunk, a lady of considerable fortune. He entered Parliament and by 1748 was President of the Board of Trade. He was a zealous promoter of English trading interests, and was described as the Father of the Colonies. The town of Halifax, Nova Scotia, was given his name. He was lord of the manor of Westbourne, to which parish he made an offer in 1770, the year before his death. The parishioners could have either a church spire or an endowment for a Sunday afternoon sermon. The choice fell on the spire, because "it would always point to Heaven whereas a sermon might not." **[30]**

ALDWICK

A Captain Allaway hoped, in the late 1920s, to make here a seaside resort different from the norm. He developed Aldwick Bay Estate, where each house should have accommodation for staff and chauffeur, and a garden large enough for a tennis court. Call it snobbery if you like, but his brochure explained that his aim was to create a quiet environment 'not invaded by trippers and charabanc parties', which would be 'free from bands, pierrot parties and the noise and hustle only too commonly associated with many seaside resorts.' He succeeded so well that the Estate became one of the South Coast havens for the theatrical lights of the day. **[25]**

ALFRISTON

Scuffles in church rarely involve the preacher, but one here did. The first minister of the chapel was a Mr. Betts, whose strict line on certain parish matters earned him the dislike of Charles Brooker, one of the Trustees. One Sunday Brooker, to get his revenge, placed an itinerant preacher in the pulpit before Mr. Betts arrived. Stanton Collins (see *Crowlink*, and Alfriston in *Hidden Sussex*) and his gang burst into the chapel, forcibly evicted the preacher and insisted on Mr. Betts mounting the steps to the pulpit. When he did they mounted guard around it. Later on the same day there was a bad thunderstorm, and Brooker held a prayer meeting in the chapel, because the people thought it was a judgment on them for the disgraceful fracas earlier.

James Harry Batho trained horses at the Wingrove Racing Stables in the early 20th century, and the whole village would share the rewards of a major victory. After Longset won the Lincoln in 1912, every Alfriston family received a joint of beef. Mr Batho was a local benefactor who organized sports meetings on the Tye. Here Horatio Bottomley (see *Upper Dicker*) would often present the prizes. **[28]**

AMBERLEY

Always the home of artists — and no wonder! Local names include those of Gerald Burn, Edward Stott, and Fred Stratton and his son Hilary, a distinguished sculptor. In earlier times, Izaak Walton, author of *The Compleat Angler,* loved the river here for its trout, and often fished in the Arun. John Pennicott, born near the end of the 18th century, was a famous Sussex musician who lived in the same Amberley house for forty years. But he seems to have got around because at different times he led the band in Henfield and Woodmancote churches — assuming, that is, that he was the only man of that name. This might be unlikely, as 'John Pennicott' played the 'clarionet' at Amberley and the trombone at Henfield! Anyhow, one day the band had had a 'difference of opinion' with the vicar at Amberley and refused to play, although they attended the service. The vicar (then over eighty years of age) asked from the pulpit, "Are you going to play or not?" Pennicott answered for them all, "No!", whereupon the vicar retorted, "Well then, I'M not going to preach", and promptly left the pulpit!

From more recent times comes the story of James Goble, son of Captain Goble who lived at Houghton Bridge: he is recorded under *Houghton.* Amberley Mount was the scene in 1909 of pioneer gliding attempts by various people, especially E.C. Gordon England, who kept his machine 'The Albatross' aloft for 58 seconds on 27 June 1909, a feat which remained the world's record for almost a decade.

An interesting brass in the church shows John Wantele, who died in 1424. It is the earliest known illustration of a tabard. Another famous name is John Ireland, the composer, of whom we wrote in *Hidden Sussex.*   **[18]**

AMBERSTONE

In 1815 all Europe was in turmoil. The Czar of Russia and the King of Prussia were both in England as refugees from the invasions of Napoleon. At one time both, with their entourages, were at Portsmouth awaiting notification for their return to the Continent. An urgent message came that they were to embark at Dover, so the Czar, King and their suites made a hurried journey by less frequented roads. They halted for refreshment at Amberstone, where a good quaker farmer named Rickman held the farm. He it was who, with almost no warning, found himself offering hospitality to two suites of itinerant royalty at the same time!   **[22]**

ANGMERING

Sixty-one years in the same parish was the achievement of the Rev. William Kinleside, Rector here from 1776 to 1836. From 1802 he was also vicar of Poling. He was very musical and played the 'cello. Often he drove in his lumbering old coach with two horses, to attend concerts at Chichester. In those days the roads were very bad and the fifteen-mile trip would take 2½ hours. One hopes that his enjoyment was proportionate to the effort involved in getting there. [26]

ANSTY

Legh Manor, with an endowment of £5,000, was presented to the Sussex Archaeological Society in 1936 by Lady Chance, in memory of her late husband, Sir William Chance, Bt. The formal opening ceremony was performed by no less a person than Sir Edward Lutyens, one of the great names in English architecture. Another Ansty opening was of the Village Hall, by Mrs. A.C. Lampson, whose husband was chairman of the Construction Committee. Nearly all the building work, amounting to 1,580 hours, was put into the project by local men.

Sir Harry Preston was a real personality of the inter-war years. He owned the Royal Albion Hotel at Brighton, and was a fine sportsman. He had for many years a little country hide-out at Ansty, called Apple Tree Cottage. [12]

APPLEDRAM

Not everyone with the wherewithal was allowed to build a castle in days gone by. Richard Ryman of Apuldram, its alternative spelling, was one of those disappointed, but the poor fellow had already acquired the stone by the time the refusal was announced: it was used instead for the bell tower near the west end of Chichester Cathedral. Near Apuldram church is a house called Rymans with a massive fifteenth-century tower of the same kind of stone. It's said that this is where Richard Ryman *would* have built his castle.

Surprisingly, Appledram had its own local doctor as long ago as 1622. His name was John Beame, but all was not well because in that year he was 'presented' — reported to the authorities — because he 'did practise physicke there' without a licence. Four years later, John Grig was also 'presented' for 'going to plow uppon Ascension day last'.

Shortly afterwards, about 1640, a family named Fowler came from the West of England to manufacture salt on the flat land near where the canal ended, and there they stayed until the last of the line, Alderman Fowler, died in 1925. He is credited with the introduction of swans to the Birdham area. [43]

ARDINGLY

Wakehurst, now owned by the National Trust, was acquired by the Sussex Culpeper family in the fifteenth century. Two sisters, Margaret and Elizabeth Wakehurst, daughters and co-heirs of Richard Wakehurst, married two brothers, Richard and Nicholas Culpeper. Richard had no issue, and Nicholas succeeded to the estate. He made up for his brother by having no fewer than eighteen children. The present Wakehurst Place was built by his descendant Sir Edward Culpeper, in 1590. In the village is a house called Culpepers, built only in 1926. The owner was Viscountess Wolseley, authoress of several books on Sussex, who died there in 1936. She was a daughter of Field-Marshal Viscount Wolseley. Among her many local benefactions was a large collection of books and other material, presented to Hove Public Library — the Lady Wolseley room there was built to house it.
[11/12]

ARLINGTON

To be hanged for theft was the fate of one John Williams in 1613. A few days after his execution his widow gave birth to a son, who was taken to Arlington church to be baptized. The church register has this entry: '14 March. Stephen, the sonne of John Williams, executed fortnight before for stealing. God give his sonne more grace.' However, misfortune attended little Stephen, too; he was buried on 18 February 1615. [22]

ASHBURNHAM

How far back can ancestry be traced? According to a persistent family tradition, at the time of the Norman Conquest Bertram, Lord of Esburnham, was High Sheriff of Sussex and Surrey, and Constable of Dover Castle. His direct descendant was John Ashburnham, Groom of the Bedchamber to Charles I. He was elected to Parliament in 1640, and remained a staunch Royalist. When in 1646 the king left Oxford in haste, he had but two attendants — John Ashburnham and a guide. At his king's execution John was given several relics, preserved in Ashburnham church until their removal in the 19th century. Among them was a watch which Ashburnham claimed was given to him by Charles I just before his execution: but see *Tillington*. [23]

ASHINGTON

Queen Elizabeth I passed through Ashington in 1591, during one of her 'progresses'. A detailed account of her visit was written in the parish register. During a lawsuit in the early eighteenth century the register was for some reason stolen and has never been recovered. Perhaps it contained some damaging entry. The rectory was a lath-and-plaster building, and to get the book the thief made a hole through the outside wall to the cupboard where the book was kept. [19]

ASHLING

West Ashling formerly could boast both a windmill and a watermill. The windmill was built about 1860; after a mere half-century of life its sweeps were removed in about 1916, but the fan remained. Then in 1922 a nearby resident complained of the noise the fan made as it revolved, so it too was removed. The watermill was built in 1825 for corn milling, and apart from a few years when it made paper pulp continued working until the 1930s. It was always known as Hackett's mill, although even Martin Brunnarius (to whose fine book we are often indebted) doesn't seem to know who Hackett was.　　[17]

ASHURST

'Michael Fairless', who wrote that delightful and profound book, *The Roadmender*, was a woman. Margaret Fairless Barber was born in Rastrick, Yorkshire, in 1869. She trained as a nurse, and worked in the Jago, one of the worst London slums. But her health gave way and after a period travelling in Germany she settled in Sussex. She died, aged only 33, at Mock Bridge near Henfield on 24 August 1901. Her grave has a wooden cross carved with a quotation from the medieval Lady Julian of Norwich. *The Roadmender* was published the year after her death.

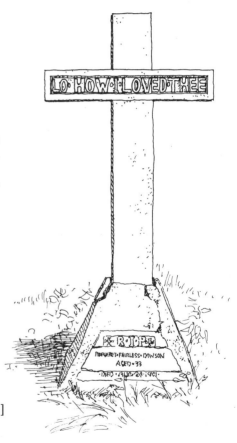

A branch of the Covert family was connected with Ashurst for over 300 years. In 1338 it was settled on Richard de Covert, and in 1671 on Ann Covert, who married Sir James Morton. The name of Covert thus died out — and so it remains, being absent even from the current Brighton telephone directory.

[10]

ASHURSTWOOD

Homestall (see *Hidden Sussex*) was originally a hunting lodge belonging to John of Gaunt. By the time of Henry VIII it had come to the Aske family. John Aske, like so many landowners of the period, was attainted of high treason, and the king confiscated it. In the twentieth century it belonged to Lord Dewar, who lived there and made the garden his chief pleasure.　　[5]

ATHERINGTON

During the Middle Ages a monastic house stood here, a daughter cell of the great Abbey of Séez in Normandy. Among the buildings was the moated house of the Bailiff of Séez, a person of some consequence whose job it was to keep a watchful eye on the possessions of the mother house. The north transept of Climping church was reserved for the Bailiff, his tenants and servants — but not, you notice, for his family, since usually he was himself a monk. The lands of Séez were confiscated by King Henry V on the outbreak of the French wars in 1415. The buildings fell into disrepair after the Dissolution of 1536, and, thanks to the inroads of the sea, by 1840 only the small private chapel was left. However, in the 1930s the whole estate belonged to Lord Moyne, previously the Hon. Walter Guinness, Minister of Agriculture in the late 1920s. He enlisted the services of the architect Amyas Phillips to recreate the old buildings. This he did with such success that, in the words of Ian Nairn, they are "in a medieval way of design which is absolutely indistinguishable from old work."   [26]

AVISFORD

Sometimes in this book we tell of people whose names have not come down to us. One such was buried here in the second century AD in a stone sepulchral case hollowed out in one piece — what is known to archaeologists as a cist. On March 31, 1817 an estate worker using a crowbar fouled something solid, which when unearthed was found to be a stone chest about four feet long. The contents were mostly pottery and glass, and some of the receptacles contained calcined bones. There were small earthenware basins, lamps, candlesticks, a glass bottle and even a pair of sandals studded with brass nails and evidently made for small and dainty feet. The cist and its contents are now in Worthing museum, but no clues have ever emerged as to the identity of the person buried with so much care and apparent affection.   [18]

BALCOMBE

Balcombe Place was a large estate in the 19th century, with its own clerk of works and estate carpenter. From 1875 to 1884 the post was ably filled by George Greenfield, who kept a diary of his daily life. It was edited by Rev. Douglas L. Secretan, Rector of Balcombe, and published in 1937. Here are a couple of typical entries:

> "1875. June 22. Went to College, Ardingly. Heard Te Deum, very good, in temporary chapel, and a sermon with which I did not agree, as the time is gone by for the people to be governed by the church, the clergyman evidently thinking he was preaching to a Spanish or Mexican congregation."

> "1877. February 8. There were about 30 persons got out at Balcombe who had been to the pantomime by train, and all quite sober."

George J. Warren was another worker at Balcombe Place. Born in 1845, he was appointed head gardener in 1870 and stayed for 33 years, gaining many successes at the principal horticultural shows over most of that time. During more than sixty years in the village, George did almost everything. He was first chairman of the Working Mens' Club, a post he retained for over thirty years. He started the local Cricket Club, the Bowling Club and the Rifle Range. He was a sidesman and lay reader of the parish church, and a parish councillor for almost a third of a century. Devotion like that was never common.

It was in the forest near Balcombe that the geologist Gideon Mantell found the bones of an iguanadon. Born in 1790, he was a man of many parts. He was a fellow of the Royal College of Surgeons and a pioneer in the study of poisons. He once saved a woman from the gallows on a charge of murdering her husband, by refuting the expert evidence brought by the prosecution. He wrote dozens of scientific works and collected uncountable geological specimens. The British Museum bought his collection for £5,000 — a huge sum in those times. He lived first in Lewes, later in Brighton, and died in 1852. [4]

BALDSLOW

Augustus J.C.Hare was lucky enough to be born in the Villa Strozzi, Rome, in 1834. He became a prolific author, especially of travel books, but his work can scarcely be called distinguished. Being a bit of a snob, he preferred to write of cosy happenings in exalted social circles. He prided himself on having famous friends; one of them, the King of Sweden, invested him with the Order of St. Olaf. He wrote *The Story of My Life* in six uneventful volumes, besides a string of guidebooks. There were eight on Italy, six on France, others on Spain, Holland and Russia, and (nearer home) Durham, Shropshire and (in 1894) Sussex. His books incorporated sizeable borrowings from other authors. The historian E.A. Freeman called him "a bare-faced robber." Even worse, he was sued for plagiarism. He died in 1903 at Holmhurst (now St. Mary's Convent), where he had lived for 12 years. [24]

BARCOMBE

Here lived George Grantham, who in the 1820s and 1830s was one of the closest friends of Dr. Gideon Mantell (see *Balcombe*). In 1831 occurs this interesting entry in Mantell's Journal: "January 9. Drove to Brighton (with my friend Mr. George Grantham) in the evening .... went to the theatre and saw Miss Fanny Kemble (for the 1st. time) as Lady Townley, her father Charles Kemble playing Lord T. ....which spoiled all my pleasure, for I could not for the life of me divest my mind of the fact that the father was playing the part of the husband to his daughter." The Kembles were at this time the leading stars of the English stage.   [21]

BARGHAM

It was formerly a distinct parish and manor, but now it's just an open (and lovely) area of the South Downs. It belonged in the thirteenth century to Hugh de Albini, the fifth Earl of Arundel (see *Introduction*). It then passed to the Tregoz family, first to John, later (in 1331) to Thomas de Tregoz, who was called to Parliament. The Tregoz family owned large areas of West Sussex (see *Wiggonholt*).   [18]

BARLAVINGTON

William Tipper and Robert Dawe came too late into the world to be given vast grants of land such as we find in Norman times. But in the reign of Elizabeth I they did pretty well. On 30 March 1592 the Queen granted them a huge list of manors and properties in Sussex, including tithes and lands here which had formerly belonged to the priory of Eartham or Herringham. There is no record of any payment, but we doubt if they received a free gift. Tipper and Dawe must have been land speculators on quite a large scale because old records show that they were selling off more large parts of the Queen's grant within a very few days, doubtless at a handsome profit.   [9]

BARNHAM

Following on from the previous entry, this was another manor which in the time of Elizabeth I was in the gift of the Crown. The Virgin Queen granted it to Sir Thomas White, who had been Lord Mayor of London. The reason for this generosity is not entirely clear, but he seems to have been a leader in putting down the Papist rebellion headed by Sir Thomas Wyatt in 1554.

Sadly, what may have been a glory of Barnham no longer exists. In 1409 a chantry was founded in the church by a local resident, John le Taverner; but it was pulled down at the Dissolution in the 1530s. It was in the north aisle, and even that has been destroyed, so that the very siting of John's chantry is unknown.   [18]

BATTLE

Elizabeth Vassall, the daughter of a wealthy West Indies planter, lived a life which wouldn't be out of place in a lurid romantic novel. Around 1780, when only fifteen, she married into the Webster family who then owned the abbey (or what remained of it) and its lands. Her bridegroom was Sir Godfrey Webster Bt., then aged about 40 and lacking in any sympathy or affection for his girl wife. They couldn't live in the abbey as it was still inhabited by his aunt, widow of the second baronet, who allowed the house to fall into complete decay and couldn't be dislodged: her nephew and his wife even faked ghosts and rattling chains at night to frighten her, but to no avail. Eventually Elizabeth, tired of her in-laws, eloped with Henry Fox, the third Lord Holland, taking her daughter Harriett with her. Being afraid that Sir Godfrey would claim the child, she concocted a story about Harriett's death from measles caught during a trip to Italy. She got the English chaplain at Leghorn to read the burial service and inter the 'child' — which was, in fact, a dead kid!

[23/24]

BAYHAM

The abbey, founded in 1208 and belonging to the Praemonstratensian order, had a number of turbulent moments before it was suppressed in 1525. In 1310, for instance, Sir Henry de Leyburne took an armed band to the gates and the abbot had to buy him off after a siege of three days. During the following year he stole the abbey's horses, and when the Pope intervened Leyburne had his messenger monk attacked and robbed. Eventually the order sent its inspectors to Bayham, the upshot being that both the abbot and Leyburne were ejected, with penances being imposed on their supporters. When Cardinal Wolsey decided that  the place was sufficiently run down to deserve suppression (he wanted to transfer the endowments to his planned colleges at Oxford and Ipswich) there was a sit-in by the canons and the abbey servants. Their revolt was defeated, however, and the ring-leaders were imprisoned. [7]

BEAUPORT

A Roman builder called Bassus, or possibly Bassianus, is the only man whose name has come down to us from what was one of the most important iron-working sites in Britain. The remains of it (deep in the woods at Beauport Park) were excavated by a former prep school headmaster Gerald Brodribb. Starting in 1966, he uncovered the outlines of a large complex of buildings, including a substantial bath-house with walls still standing to a height of seven feet in places. The bath-house would have been at least some consolation for Romans living far from home in a desolate, cold and muddy spot. And Bassus? A fragment of an inscription was unearthed which suggests that he was the agent in charge of the bath-house extension. Judging by the quality of the additional rooms, Brodribb has written, 'he seems to have been an early jerry-builder'. [24]

BECKLEY

It's said that after the murder of Thomas a Becket one of the four knights, Sir Reginald Fitz-Urse, was overcome by conscience and spurred his horse at a gallop for the sanctuary of Beckley. Alas for him, the rule of sanctuary didn't apply to the crimes of treason and sacrilege, and he was captured. Legend claims that even now, on dark nights along the road at Beckley, you can hear the hoofs of the ghostly horse of Sir Reginald as he once again seeks sanctuary. [15]

BEDDINGHAM

Once upon a time, it seems, the awarding of honours was a thought more capricious than it is today. Thomas Carr, a local man, was deputed to carry to George III an address congratulating the king on his providential escape when fired upon during a visit to the theatre. At once the king bestowed a knighthood on him.

John Hoper, who built Asham House in the parish, decided to oversee the work himself. He became puzzled at the slowness of progress: yet the men were apparently working steadily, even when he arrived unheralded, and even though he used a variety of routes. The truth was that the workmen spent a lot of time playing cricket. They put a boy to watch on the high ground behind, who gave a signal whenever he saw Hoper approaching. [21]

BELLS YEW GREEN

Roger Breecher, an ironmaster here, died in 1567 leaving a will written in the most extraordinary mixture of French and English. *Frant*, by Patricia Wright, is one of the best and most entertaining village histories we've read, and from it we take the words which he used to surrender 'le forge, lez measons lez forgerers do inhabit, lez coleplaces et lez wast parcells pour lez cinder, lez shoppes et pur carriageis la auters cha'ars necessaries'. [6]

BEPTON

One of the candidates for the title "England's least successful philosopher" must surely be Herbert Spencer, who made Bepton Rectory his summer home for several years. Born in 1820, he published the first of a long series of books in 1851. He developed a theory of evolutionary philosophy in which a Law of Physical Evolution led on to an ethical system. The latter, as Spencer himself admitted, was only partially successful. His ideas soon lost favour, and Thomas Carlyle called him "the most immeasurable ass in Christendom." We doubt if today he's read by anyone except students. [8]

BERSTED, SOUTH

Here are the graves of two notable sons of Sussex. Sir Richard Hotham spent a fortune trying to develop Bognor as the West Sussex rival to Brighton, but with incomplete success. He even tried to get the town's name changed to Hothampton. Also here lies William Ward Higgs, a Victorian musician now known for a single work — his song *Sussex by the Sea*. He lived for most of his life in a Victorian house in the village.   [18/26]

BERWICK

At the battle of Lewes on 14 May 1264 the last man to keep the field was Philip Basset, Lord of Berwick and a stout champion of the king's cause. He was captured, put in the custody of Simon, the son of Simon de Montfort, and taken to Dover Castle.

Later there came to live at Mays, to the north-east of Selmeston, John Nutt. He was both patron and parson of Berwick in the early seventeenth century. In 1619 he began his *Rememberances of the Parsons of Barwick*, an account of day-to-day affairs in his parish. His son, sometimes called 'the notorious Sir Thomas Nutt', was a JP feared for his harsh enforcement of the laws against nonconformists.

In the 20th century Berwick church has been the scene of a revival of the old art of wall-painting, by the Bloomsbury Group whom we recorded in *Hidden Sussex*. The pulpit is especially gay with its swags and flowers.   [28]

BIGNOR

Edward Hasler, an ardent Royalist who became rector of Bignor in 1631, ran into trouble with the Cromwellians in 1642. According to a report in 1714, he was "sent up for to *London*, upon some *Accusations* against him: one of which, more particularly, was his *Reading the Homilies*. In return to which, when he answered, that he had read but one, which was that against *Rebellion*; he was for that *sawcy Reply* turned out of his Rectory, and afterwards lived in great Poverty until the *Restoration*; when he recovered his *Living* again out of the Hands of the Usurper, one *Peeos*, who was esteemed by all, a Rank Knave". The real name of the improbable Peeos was Thomas Reaves!

A near native of Bignor was Charlotte Smith, born 1749; a prolific authoress of novels long forgotten, and poetry of some quality, likewise in limbo. At 15 she married Benjamin Smith, a profligate who gave her twelve children, broken health and precious little affection. She died in October 1806. A few lines of hers are printed under *Middleton*.

The name of farmer Tupper is recorded as being that of the discoverer of the Roman villa whose extensive mosaics constitute one of the county's great art treasures. What is less known is that the site of the villa, nearly 170 years later, still belongs to the Tupper family, direct descendants of George Tupper and proud of their long inheritance. [18]

BILLINGSHURST

Another story of religious strife has received worthy commemoration. The Rev. William Wilson, MA of Cambridge University, was ejected from the living of the parish of Billingshurst on August 24, 1662, in consequence of the so-called Act of Uniformity passed in May that year. It was intended to re-establish the episcopal form of worship and the Book of Common Prayer after the Puritan dissensions of Oliver Cromwell's time. Several warrants were issued for Wilson's arrest, but he was never found. He was given refuge in the house of a Dr. Banks, a clergyman who (unlike Wilson) had accepted the Established Church and the Revised Prayer Book of 1662. Wilson died in 1670, aged about 40, but was not forgotten. On September 16, 1912 a service commemorating his ejectment was held in Trinity Congregational Church, Billinghurst, when a tablet was unveiled to him recording 'his faithfulness to the claims of conscience.'

'Mark Rutherford' (William Hale White, 1831-1913) was a prolific writer as well as being assistant director of contracts at the Admiralty. Under his real name he published translations of works by Spinoza, and studies of Wordsworth and Bunyan. He was the son of a dissenting minister, and himself preached on more than one occasion in the Unitarian Chapel here. [10]

BINDERTON

The ivy-clad ruin we mentioned in *Hidden Sussex* is no longer ivy-clad: it's being restored as we write this entry. But we've unearthed a puzzle about the story of a burial in unhallowed ground. Somewhere we read that the ground was never consecrated; but in 1535 one Robert Cobden made a will giving to his 'own parish church' twenty pence and 'to our Lady of the same', three shillings. As Cobden lived at Binderton a century before William Smith, presumably the land on which the chapel stood must have been dedicated after all.

Here too lived Simon Eden, son of Anthony Eden, Prime Minister and later Lord Avon. Simon was killed while serving as a Pilot Officer in the RAF: his name appears on the War Memorial in the parish church of West Dean.

[17]

BINSTED

When the church was restored in 1867, some remarkable wall paintings were found. Among them was a twelfth century figure of a queen over whose head were the letters STA MARG. This seems to refer to Queen Margaret of Scotland who had been canonized shortly before the date of this painting (c.1140). If so, Binsted has a truly unique work of art, since no other portrayal of her is known. It is noted in *Memorials of Old Sussex* (London, G. Allen, 1909) that evidence once existed connecting the Queen with a local family, which might account for the presence of this unlikely figure in a remote Sussex church. [18/26]

BIRCHGROVE

A hamlet which grew around the great house of the same name, not far from Horsted Keynes. The house belongs to the Macmillan family, publishers, and the most eminent member of the clan lives there now. He is the Earl of Stockton, formerly Mr. Harold Macmillan, MP and eventually Prime Minister. [5]

BIRDHAM

We can't provide the name, but we know that an irascible old man used to play the violin for church services here, hidden away in the musicians' gallery. Once he was playing for a service with enormous gusto when a fiddle-string broke. Exasperated beyond control, he threw the instrument from the gallery down into the middle of the nave and shouted, 'Goo down theer and bide theer!' And he refused to play ever again.

More seriously, William Roebuck Read came to live at Mill House in July 1922, having retired from business in the City of London. He kept notes of the local flora and fauna he observed and in mid-1926 published his records — there was a revised edition in 1928. Though he denied having any scientific expertise, he was a most careful observer. In under six years he recorded sightings of 15 different mammals, 75 species of birds, and over 100 wild plants and flowers, all close to the Chichester basin.   [25]

BIRLING

Parson Jonathan Darby and his wife lie in the churchyard at *East Dean*, under which head we tell their story. Darby's cave, immediately below Belle Tout lighthouse, was washed away by the sea a century ago. After Darby's death in October 1726 a hundred years elapsed before any remedy was sought for the continuing tragedies under the cliffs. Then in 1828 a small wooden hut for a lookout and light was erected as an experiment at Belle Tout. It led to the building, six years later, of the revolutionary (as it then was) permanent lighthouse *(picture on p.17)*. The designer, William Hallett, a well-known architect, utilized the durable Aberdeen stone, brought by barges to Maidstone and thence dragged across the Downs by teams of oxen. The site was 334 feet above high water mark, and the building another 47 feet above that. The light revolved once in two minutes; its beam, supplied by thirty oil lamps in reflectors, could be seen twenty-three miles out to sea.   [28]

BISHOPSTONE

From 1791 to 1800 the rector here was local poet James Hurdis. His father, also James, was Collector of Customs, Newhaven; he died in 1769. Our James was born at Bishopstone in 1763, and died there in 1801, aged 38. In 1793, when only 30, he was elected Professor of Poetry at Oxford. His longest poem, *The Village Curate*, published in 1788, preceded *Favourite Village*, about Bishopstone; a poem not completely forgotten for a century and more. But Hurdis' poetic talent was limited. For instance, from *The Village Curate*:

> *A bird's nest. — Mark it well, within, without;*
> *No tool had he that wrought, no knife to cut,*
> *No nail to fix, no bodkin to insert,*
> *No glue to join; his little beak was all;*
> *And yet how neatly finished! . . .*   [27]

BLACKBOYS

Many of the older generation must remember Ronald Shiner, the actor who made such a hit in *Worm's Eye View* and other West End farces in the 1950s. He retired from the stage while still comparatively young and took over as landlord of the inn here. **[13]**

BLACKDOWN

Aldworth House, on the slopes of Blackdown Hill, was built for Lord Tennyson, whose previous home on the Isle of Wight was becoming the focus of too much attention from prying eyes. He lived here for the last 22 years of his life, perhaps the most famous poem of the Aldworth years being *Crossing the Bar*. The first year of his marriage had been spent in Sussex with less happy results. (See *Warninglid*). **[1]**

BLACKSTONE

Sir Edwin Lutyens was commissioned to design Blackstone Grange as a wedding present just before the first world war — but the young couple were destined never to live there. It was built by a Mr Miller for his son and prospective daughter-in-law. The young man failed to return from the war and Mr Miller himself lived at the Grange instead.

Note, a little way down the lane, the old village well, unheralded on the verge. **[20]**

BOARSHEAD

At Renby Hall (better known as Renby Place) secret radio broadcasts were made to France during 1940. Among those whose voices were heard was Virginia Woolf, who refers to the experience in her letters and in her diary. **[6]**

BODIAM

Jack Fuller (see *Brightling*) saved Bodiam Castle from demolition, but two later owners actually spent a lot of money on restoring it. In 1864 George Cubitt bought it for 'something over £5,000' and had got through another £40,000 or so by 1907. His son Thomas sold it to the Marquis Curzon of Kedleston, who in 1926 produced a superb history of the castle. He sold most of the estate but kept 50 acres 'in order to make a worthy setting for the castle, which I had resolved to restore with a view to presenting it ultimately to the nation'. This he did, and happily it's still a breathtaking spectacle. **[15]**

BOLNEY

Wykehurst was built in the 1870s for Henry Huth, probably the greatest book-collector of his day (see *Hidden Sussex*). His library was eventually dispersed; the sale of the bulk of it in 1910 fetched no less than £300,000. His son Austin was born in 1881, became an army captain in the 1914-18 War, and was killed during the epic struggle for Hill 60 on April 20, 1915. His brother Edward in 1905 gave the church its fine lych-gate.

Something in Bolney air seems to breed giants. Henry Blaker was born here in 1724, and at age eighteen was 7ft. 4in. tall. He was shown in London as 'The British Giant, the tallest man ever seen.' In 1734 Bolney saw the funeral of Henry Lintott, 'the largest man that ever was seen.'[11]

BOREHAM STREET

In 1688 John Benbrigg (or Benbridge) married Mary Creed. Benbrigg was a 'Boram' man of substance, who in middle life bought a house here. It's now part of the White Friars Hotel. Over the garden door, once the house front door, is a carved stone bearing the date 1721 and the initials B over I M — i.e., Benbrigg, John, Mary.

[23]

BOSHAM

Earl Godwine of the Anglo-Saxons was a native of Sussex, perhaps even of Bosham. His father Wulfnoth, the Anglo-Saxon Chronicle relates, was the Sussex thegn whose piratical activities destroyed the fleet of King Ethelred. Godwine himself was wealthy, gifted with great eloquence, and completely lacking in scruple. On the death of Canute in 1035, Harold I was by popular desire elevated to the throne, although within a few years Godwine by guile and treachery became the chief power in the land. But the two sons of Emma of Normany, queen of Ethelred II, also laid claim to the English throne. The younger son, Alfred, landed hereabouts in 1036 to visit his mother at Winchester. Godwine intercepted him, putting him and his retinue brutally to death. Godwine's final bid for power came in 1049, when at Bosham his elder son Swegen murdered his cousin Beorn. Godwine was outlawed for his treachery, but in 1050 his earldom was restored to him. Then in 1051 he was again banished from England, returning to Sussex the following year. The sorry tale ended at Hastings in 1066 with the extinction of Earl Godwine and his line. [30]

BOTOLPHS

According to a recent tally there are nearly a hundred churches up and down the country dedicated to this 7th century saint, though his equally saintly brother Adulf notches up hardly any. After being educated on the continent, he was given a barren and water-logged piece of ground somewhere along the east coast of England. He began to build an abbey in 654 AD, and remained there until he died in 680. When the place was destroyed during the Danish invasions the remains of both brothers were preserved and distributed around various abbeys as relics. [19/20]

BOXGROVE

In the Easter 'presentments' of 1662 Anthony Ward and Edward Hartley were accused of playing cricket during the time of evensong on Sunday April 28. Worse, on the following Sunday Hartley was again accused of playing cricket, with others named and unnamed, in the churchyard, aided and abetted by the two churchwardens. Of course the fashion for tombstones hadn't really got under way in 1662 or the great game would have resembled nothing so much as an obstacle race.

Colin Pullinger, born in the village in 1815, was the inventor of an improved beetle trap, a self-acting cinder sifter and, most notably, a humane mouse-trap which was automatically reset by each new captive. [17]

BRAMBER

Fleeing to France after the battle of Worcester, Charles the Second had a close shave at Bramber. He was riding, disguised, towards the south coast with Lord Wilmot and Colonel George Gounter of Racton House near Chichester on the afternoon of October 14, 1651. 'Being come to Bramber,' Gounter recorded later, 'we found the streets full of soldiers both sides the houses.' Wilmot was all for turning back, but Gounter and the king thought they would attract less attention by continuing. Just as they thought the danger was over they heard a ferocious clatter of hooves and between 30 and 40 soldiers poured past them, almost toppling them from their saddles. They spent the night at Brighton and the king escaped the next morning from Shoreham. (See also *Houghton*).

Walter Potter (1835-1918) had an unusual cast of mind. He delighted in collecting animal freaks — lambs with two heads, chickens with four legs and so on — and, as he was a taxidermist, stuffing them. But he began his most creative work after looking through his sister's nursery-rhyme book. He started making ambitious tableaux, such as The Original Death and Burial of Cock Robin and The House that Jack Built. He also adapted scenes from local life, among them The Guinea Pigs' Cricket Match, The Rabbits' Village School and The Kittens' Wedding. Potter's Victorian amassing of the weird and wonderful is still intact and on view, though it has moved to Arundel. [19]

BREDE

The gunpowder industry claimed several lives in this part of Sussex and the Sussex Weekly Advertiser's report of the last explosion at Brede gunpowder mill in 1808 makes harrowing reading (we spare you the worst): 'One of the men named Sinden, at work in the sifting house, had his head and limbs separated from his body and carried in different directions to a neighbouring wood wherein they were collected and placed together and presented a shocking spectacle.' (See also *Sedlescombe*).

We told the story of Sir Goddard Oxenbridge in *Hidden Sussex*. The place of his legendary death is still called Groaning Bridge, but he wasn't the only noteworthy person of this family. The Oxenbridges appear to have originated in Rye, but acquired Brede Place in the 15th century. One, John Oxenbridge, was a canon of St George's Chapel, Windsor, in the early 16th century and he founded a chantry there. A later John, who died in 1617, was a well-known Puritan preacher. A branch of the family emigrated and settled in New England. Although the name has died out in this country we're told by M.A. Lower that at least in the late 19th century it was still extant in the USA (and see *Guestling*).

The actress Dame Ellen Terry, who lived at Winchelsea, often came to Brede, in whose church precincts she would partake of a solitary picnic lunch. She's said to have remarked that it was the most cheerful churchyard she had ever known! As we referred to the museum-like quality of Brede Church in our earlier volume we were amused to find a similar comment (but less kindly meant) in the Sussex County Magazine of February 1932. Dean Swift's cradle was at that time to be found in the church, having been bought at a Brighton curio sale and given to Canon Frewer who thought the church should have it unless any Dublin interests should make a large offer for it. The writer E.V. Lucas called it an 'alien curiosity' and the magazine's editor commented that 'there is something incongruous in the fact that a Sussex church houses the infant bed of the author of Gulliver's Travels and in so doing takes on the character of a museum'. Where is it now?

Among the 'exhibits' in the church today is a madonna carved from the trunk of an oak by Clare Sheridan, who lived at Brede Place. **[24]**

BRIGHTLING

We trust we shall be forgiven for saying a few words more about the eccentric John Fuller, despite giving him a good mention in *Hidden Sussex*. 'Mad Jack' he may have been to his detractors, and nicknamed 'the Hippopotamus' because of his size, but he was 'Honest Jack' in his own estimation and actually turned down the offer of a peerage by Pitt. A Member of Parliament, he was once forcibly ejected from the House for calling the Speaker 'an insignificant little fellow in a wig'. He's best known for his follies, but he encouraged the arts and sciences and saved Bodiam Castle from being broken up by a builder as a stone quarry.

It would be wrong, however, to suggest that Mad Jack is the only notable to have been connected with the village. William of Wykeham, for instance, was rector here in 1362, before going on to Winchester. In the church there's a bust of the composer William Shield (1748-1829), a boat-builder's apprentice who rose to become Master of the King's Musick, was a friend of

Haydn and wrote several songs which, to quote the *Oxford Companion to Music*, 'will long be relished by simple-minded music-lovers'.

In the churchyard look out for a cast-iron grave slab to Nicholas Russell. He's remembered because this is, according to all the records, the very last iron grave-slab made in Sussex.

[14]

BROADBRIDGE HEATH

A tale here of a poisoned pudding and wifely murder. In August 1750 James and Ann Whale came to live in the village, sharing a house with James and Sarah Pledge. Whale and Mrs Pledge fell out and he banned her from his part of the house. It seems that Ann Whale was none too enamoured of her husband, either, since Sarah Pledge suggested to her that they 'get rid of this devil' by poisoning him. She set off on a long and unfruitful search to Dorking, Rusper and Horsham before baking some spiders and putting them in beer for Whale to drink. Ann apparently found the bottle and threw it away. Then Mrs Pledge made a pudding for him, into which she popped some 'white mercury', and he died the next day. That, at least, was Ann's story. Sarah Pledge, not surprisingly, declared before the justices that Ann had begged her to get the poison and that Ann had done all the dirty work with the pudding. But the tale and counter-tale didn't do either of them any good, for on July 24, 1752, they were both executed — Ann by burning, Sarah by hanging. [3]

BROAD OAK

In 1816 the most important house in the village was taken on lease by John Francis, who set up a boarding school named The Broad Oak Academy. At one time it had 40 boarders and some 60 day scholars of both sexes, most of them children of prosperous farmers and tradesmen. However, in 1829 an outbreak of smallpox among the children caused the Academy to be closed down, and Mr Francis moved over the county boundary to Cranbrook. Before his departure he issued a handbill of curious nature, defending himself comprehensively against charges of negligence and concealment which had been spread around. Printed in a welter of different type faces, which we can't attempt to reproduce, it began: 'J. Francis....has deeply to lament, that after a residence at Broad Oak for about 13 years, there should be found one individual so totally unacquainted with his true character, as to suppose him capable of endeavouring to conceal such a dreadful disease in his House, and thereby expose his Neighbours and nearly a hundred children under his Tuition to its direful contagion...'   [13]

BROADWATER

John Mapilton was a 15th century priest as well as being a most learned lawyer. He gained considerable favour with Henry IV and was Chancellor to his Queen, Margaret of Anjou, niece of the King of France. Mapilton died in 1432, and there's a brass to him in Broadwater church, where he was buried.
                                                                        [26]

BUCKS GREEN

We confess ourselves suckers for naive versifying, as testified by several examples in this book. In his *West Sussex Village Book* Tony Wales celebrates the life of Percy Naldrett, who was a friend of Hilaire Belloc. He worked in Bucks Green as a printer and was also a conjurer, book collector and keen motorcyclist who took his aged sister for a rural spin when he was nearly 80. On his 85th birthday he wrote a poem which was read at his funeral four months later:

> Farewell dear Sussex, the place that gave me birth,
> Farewell to my beloved Downs,
> Farewell to golden Weald with jewelled earth,
> With snuggling inns and lovely ancient towns   [3]

BULVERHYTHE

This area on the top of the cliffs west of St Leonards is nowadays a fully developed residential suburb of Hastings. Not so in 1335, when John de Bretagne owned the manor, a ferry across Bulverhythe Water (presumably income-producing on a small scale) and lands which included, astonishingly, no less than twenty acres of salt pasture. John was evidently anxious for the welfare of his manor, because in 1310 he had petitioned for, and been granted, a market every Monday and an annual fair, lasting four days, around Lady Day.   [24]

BUNCTON

In 791 AD Ealdwulf was 'heretoga' (a kind of chief) of the South Saxons. He made a gift of land to the church, including in the deed the rather portentous lines: 'Whosoever may be willing to augment and amplify the bounty of this small donation, may God augment his share in the Book of Life. But if, which God forbid, anyone relying on tyrannous power should wish rashly to withhold or diminish it, let him know that on the trial of the terrible Day of Judgment he will fall with horror into the hands of the living God. Moreover this has been transacted on the hill called Biohchandune in the year of our Lord Jesu Christ 791.' The identity of the hill remained a mystery until about a century ago, when the similarity of the old and new names brought about the identification. **[19]**

BURPHAM

At around eight o'clock on the evening of September 26, 1770, William Bowles the postboy was robbed of the mail and £120 in bank bills while crossing the Downs to Steyning. Two men were involved, but only one was brought to book — Jack Upperton, who was sentenced to be hanged 'and afterwards let him be hung in chains on the nearest convenient spot upon Burpham Down nearest to the gate at the end of Blakehurst Lane, near Arundel'. Folk memory kept knowledge of the location alive and in the early 1950s local people erected an oak board on an iron post. It was about 18 inches long and carried the carving of a double gallows, the initials JU and the date, 1771. Unfortunately, it recently succumbed to the ravages of time; but we have reason to hope that it may soon be replaced — it's a shame to let the old traditions die. The place is high on the Downs and overgrown with hazel shrub.

Tribute should be paid here to the Rev. Robert Foster, who as vicar devoted 48 years to renovating the church, which he found in a deplorable condition, with no proper flooring and ivy growing in the chancel. Today it's one of the 'top ten' in Sussex, in our opinion, and the west window was fittingly erected in his memory in 1899, the year after he died. It was designed by the great stained glass artist C.E. Kempe. **[18]**

BURTON

There's a most odd painting of St Wilgefortis in the church here, but even odder is the fact that she never existed! You can read more detail about her in *The Oxford Dictionary of Saints*, but let it suffice that she was supposed to have been martyred by her father, a king of Portugal, and while on the cross she prayed that all who remembered her in their prayers should be freed from all incumbrances. She was therefore given the inelegant second name of 'St. Uncumber'. Later she became a sort of patron saint for wives who wanted to be rid of unloved husbands. So we wonder whether the Burton painting was commissioned, or even executed, by a thankful lady whose prayer to St Wilgefortis was answered. **[9]**

BURWASH

Some excellent Puritan names in Burwash, thanks to one Goddard Hepden. He had ten children and among their names were such beauties as Fearnot, Thankfull, Hopestill and Goodgift. The last named (a female) was to marry Zabulon Newington of Ticehurst, and it's rather difficult to imagine their fireside conversations with a straight face.

The most famous inhabitant of the village was Rudyard Kipling (see *Hidden Sussex*) but we'd like to give a brief mention to two other local notables: George Watson who, despite being described as 'totally illiterate and almost idiotic', became a celebrated lightning calculator and memorist; and the Rev. John Coker Egerton, author of one of the most entertaining books on Sussex ever written, *Sussex Folk and Sussex Ways*. He was the rector here from 1867 to 1888.   **[14]**

BURY

The women of Bury seem to have been made of stern stuff in former times, being renowned for both cricket and, amazingly, boxing. On June 18, 1793, the married women of the village played the maidens on Bury Common and won by 80 runs. The Bury women earned such renown that they offered to play any village eleven in the county. At about the same time crowds turned up to watch two women boxers who assumed the names of Big Ben and Mendoza. For the record, Big Ben was the winner.   **[18]**

BUXTED

Here's evidence that you can, indeed, die of a broken heart. Shortly before Mary Relfe and James Atkinson were to be married, in December 1742, a messenger arrived to tell James that his fiancée was dangerously ill. He hastened down to Buxted, where the sight of him partially revived her. She lingered for two days, constantly nursed by her beloved, but died on the Sunday evening — on which day he took to his bed, sick in body but even more sick at heart. He lay there for seven days praying for death, and died at the same hour in the evening as Mary, exactly a week later, and on the day that she was buried. He was then buried on the very day they were to have been married, and they lie side by side in the churchyard. The story was told by Mr Mitchell, the then rector of Maresfield, in a note in Latin in the parish register.   **[13]**

BYWORTH

One of the great garden experts, Patrick Synge lived at Byworth Edge for 17 years. Synge, who died in 1982, took part in many expeditions, bringing back exotic plants including (his own speciality) lilies. He worked for the Royal Horticultural Society for a quarter of a century, wrote several books and completed the work on the great RHS *Dictionary of Gardening* in four volumes.   **[9]**

CADE STREET

Jack Cade's rebellion of 1450 is summarised in *Hidden Sussex*, and there isn't much more to Cade Street than that. Cade is usually called 'of Heathfield', and nobody knows whether he took his name from the hamlet or whether the hamlet was named after him, as he was captured and killed here. He became something of a folk hero even in his lifetime. He was accused of resorting to books on magic, and of raising the Devil in the form of a black dog. His enemies naturally embroidered the stories, but even his followers felt that he had magical powers, even if they let him down at the end.

Cade was traditionally supposed to have been playing bowls in the garden of an alehouse when his pursuer Alexander Iden came upon him and shot him with an arrow. The monument in our picture was provided in the early 19th century by Francis Newbery, who then owned Heathfield Park; he was a druggist with premises in St. Paul's Churchyard, London. [13]

CAKEHAM

St. Richard de Wyche often resided at the episcopal manor house, and several miracles are related of him while there. One February 2, (the Feast of the Purification of the Virgin Mary, often called Candlemas), the saint went in procession, all the company carrying lighted candles. Suddenly a gust of wind blew out all the candles. A moment later, to everyone's surprise, Richard's candle relit itself. He asked those around who had lit it, but no-one had. He bade them all keep silence about the event, but clearly someone disobeyed him, or we should not know the story today. [25]

CAMBER

The last occasion on which a life was lost during a smuggling affray on the Sussex coast was in 1838, when a poor fiddler named Monk was shot dead by the coastguard at Camber Castle. [16]

CATSFIELD

The oldest tombstone in the church is of the 'virtuous and pious' Lady Pelham, who died in 1686. We tell something of the family in our introduction. In 1412 Sir John Pelham was granted the manor of Crowhurst by Henry IV. In 1584 Edmund Pelham extended their estates into the manor of Catsfield, but life wasn't free of ruffles: in 1593 his wife Ellen was hauled before the courts and tried 'for not frequenting the church'.

Lady Gibbs, who lived at Catsfield Place in the late 18th century, found herself the custodian of Marie Antoinette's valuables. When things became hot in France during the Revolution the Princesse de Lamballes brought the jewels to England and left them with Lady Gibbs (a friend of hers) until such time as Marie Antoinette could collect them herself — which, of course, she never did. It's been suggested that the Princess's visit was in fact a blind, masking an appeal for help from the British Government for the French royal family. Whatever the truth of the matter, she returned to France and was executed in 1792.

Thomas Brassey was a famous contractor who retired to Catsfield in 1865 after a lifetime constructing railways in the Crimea, Canada and India as well as in Britain, Denmark, Italy and other parts of Europe. He bought a large area of land and built a French-style château here which he called Normanhurst Court, though he died before it was completed. His son Thomas, who was knighted in 1881, made a peer in 1886 and created Earl Brassey in 1911, was Liberal MP for Hastings for some 20 years, a Civil Lord of the Admiralty and Lord Warden of the Cinque Ports. Normanhurst Court was demolished in 1954, but a large stone carved window survives most bizarrely in a small house at the foot of All Saints Street in Hastings. The first Thomas Brassey is commemorated in the west window of Catsfield church, the Earl's pew being below it.   [23]

CHAILEY

As book-lovers ourselves, we're pleased to record the collecting habit of John Kember (died in the 1820s), described in Horsfield's *History of the Environs of Lewes* as a man 'of very reserved habits and great eccentricity'. One of Horsfield's friends was taken aback to find in a bookseller's 'a plain and meanly dressed farmer' bargaining for a copy of Macklin's Bible published at 80 guineas. This was Kember, who was seen to put the six weighty volumes into a sack and swing the load onto the back of his old cart horse, he himself walking home to Chailey alongside, content. His house was stacked not only with books but with scientific instruments — theodolites, telescopes, protractors, quadrants, planetariums and orreries. At his death everything was sold at an auction in Lewes.   [12]

CHALVINGTON

Few early church registers have survived, mainly because they were written on perishable paper. When Queen Elizabeth I ordered that all registers were to be transcribed onto parchment, Thomas Cartwright copied the Chalvington records in beautiful handwriting into a new register book. The church guide leaflet, to which we owe thanks, reprints his 'preface'. After the usual title, he continued, 'newe wrytten by Thomas Cartwright, Parson of Eckington als Ripe ... the 22nd. day of February, ano dom 1583 because the other was decayed and very imparfytt yet kept to be seen because they may be examined together by any that be dysposed to fine faulte therewith. T.C.'[22]

CHANCTONBURY

When we told the story of Chanctonbury Ring in *Hidden Sussex* a correspondent wrote rightly telling us that the Ring is the earthwork, not the clump of trees. All the same, the Ring visible for miles around is the group of trees planted by Charles Goring in 1760, when he was only nineteen. Nearly seventy years later he wrote a poem about his scheme. We quote part of it:

> *"How oft around thy Ring, sweet Hill,*
> *A boy, I used to play,*
> *And form my plans to plant thy top*
> *On some auspicious day ...*
>
> *With what delight I placed those twigs*
> *Beneath thy maiden sod;*
> *And then an almost hopeless wail*
> *Would creep within my breast.*
> *Oh! could I live to see thy top*
> *In all its beauty dress'd.*
>
> *That time's arrived; I've had my wish,*
> *And lived to eighty-five ..."*   [19]

CHARLESTON

The Norman manor house had been much altered over the centuries and by 1930 was in a poor state. In 1931 it was bought by Sir Oswald Birley, the distinguished portrait painter; he commissioned local architect Walter Godfrey to restore it, which he did with great success. A vast barn alongside the house became the painter's studio. At one end he built a stage which could double as a dais, and informal performances were given of music, plays and pantomimes. After World War II, during which it housed numbers of soldiers from various countries, Lady Birley acted as hostess for much of the annual Sussex Festival. When that lapsed, she raised funds to use the barn for a regular Charleston Festival which began in 1968 and was continued for a good few years.   [21]

CHARLTON

Charlton Forest was a centre for smugglers and gangs of bandits. One of the most notorious was known simply as Perin; he was a native of Chichester and a respected master carpenter. He lost the use of his right hand by a palsy, and had to turn to other ways of earning his living. So he started to buy up French imported goods for the smugglers, of whom there were plenty. One day, however, his cutter was taken by Revenue Officers off the Sussex coast with a full cargo of brandy, tea and rum. It was hauled off to Poole in Dorset.

In consequence, on Sunday, October 4, 1747, a meeting of the 'Hawkhurst Gang', a much-feared band of ruffians, took place at Charlton, where Perin incited them all to a raid on Poole Customs House. Thomas Kingsmill, notorious as a ringleader in these exploits, led the attack on Poole, where they arrived at 11 p.m. The attack was successful and much of the impounded booty was recovered. But later the participants were captured and executed for their crimes. Perin was betrayed by one of his own gang, and was taken and convicted. This finally broke up the Hawkhurst Gang; those who escaped execution made their getaway to France or Holland.

In the great days of the Charlton Hunt the Master was Mr. Roper, who died in April 1715, while riding with the hounds at the age of 84. He incurred the displeasure of the Duke of Somerset, then lord of Petworth, who decided to set up a rival hunt when he saw the Charlton horses and hounds on his lands. He tried to tempt the Sussex gentry away from Charlton by fetching top-grade cooks down from London to prepare sumptuous breakfasts, but to no avail, and after a few years' vain attempts to establish his own hunt he abandoned his idea and even gave away all his hounds. [17]

CHELWOOD GATE

Robert Cecil, third son of the third Marquis of Salisbury, was born in 1864. After being a government Minister in the 1914-1918 War, he became Lord Privy Seal in 1923, and in the same year was created Viscount Cecil of Chelwood. He went on to hold several high offices, including becoming a leading proponent of the League of Nations. He joined General Smuts in preparing a draft scheme for the League in 1919, and by 1931 he felt able to tell the League Assembly that war had hardly ever been less likely than it was then. Unluckily for him, exactly eight days later Japanese forces invaded Manchuria and the world was no longer at peace. But Lord Cecil never lost hope. He lived at Chelwood Gate for much of his life and died in 1958 at the ripe age of 94. [12]

CHIDDINGLY

Was King Edward the Second a lie-a-bed? Nicholas de la Beche, who held the manor of Chiddingly as well as several others in the early 14th century, is on record as having received the considerable sum of £20 in 1311 for helping 'in the singular service of dragging the King out of bed on Easter Monday'. More we do not know!

In the south transept of the church is a monument to the Jefferay family, about whom there's a decidedly odd story. The principal figure in the monument is that of Sir John Jefferay, whose birth doesn't appear to be recorded: it was probably around 1520. He was called to the Bar in 1546 and in the 1570s became a judge and soon after Chief Baron of the Court of Exchequer. He had only one child, a daughter Elizabeth, who married Sir Edward Montague. In the monument Sir John lies in full legal regalia above his wife, while their daughter and son-in-law stand on either side on shallow drums. But what are those drums? According to tradition, when the Montagues went to church from their stately Chiddingly Place home which Sir John had built, cheeses were placed before them for use as stepping-stones to prevent their feet from getting wet in the mud! So these drums may be flat round cheeses.

In about 1880 the cottage called Cordwainers was the home of the Russells — a family which also owned adjoining Yew Tree Cottage and Thorn House. They went on, a few years later, to start a shoe retailing business which was to reach national proportions under the name Russell & Bromley.

Pablo Picasso twice stayed at the Chiddingly home of the British surrealist artist and art collector Sir Roland Penrose. The locals say that on one occasion the great Spanish painter wandered into the village pub without any cash in his pocket and offered to dash off a sketch for the landlord in payment for his drink. Being the no-nonsense type, this stolid citizen refused ('I don't care if you're Michelangelo...').

Sir Roland had a wicked sense of humour. The Royal Academy once declined one of his paintings because it incorporated a poem with a swear word in it; he successfully submitted another which showed hands signalling a four-letter word in deaf-and-dumb sign language.   [22]

CHIDHAM

Farmer Woods was the man who made Chidham famous for his wheat; his story is told in *Hidden Sussex*. But we also found a very offbeat story about Westbourne parish, which includes Chidham. Besides Westbourne parish church, there used to be three parochial chapels. One was the Hermitage, where dwelt Simon Cotes (see *Westbourne*). The second was at Prinsted, the third at Nutbourne. As to the last of these, all record has been lost, of even the site and the dedication. Its very existence is known only through the will of one Edward Esop of Chidham, dated June 2, 1538, in which he bequeaths 'to the chapel at Nutbourne 12d'. Three vanished chapels in one parish is enough! [30]

CHILGROVE

A branch of the Morley family, which originated in Suffolk, settled here in the Civil War time. The first John Morley, from Halnaker, had a son, Sir William, who made a substantial contribution to the cost of raising an army to quell the Irish rebellion of 1642. His nephew, Sir John Morley of 'Brooms' in Chilgrove, was less forthcoming. He was summoned before Parliament on November 1, 1642, as a 'delinquent' for 'refusing to contribute to the public charge in this time of common danger'. He was fined £500 for his additional delinquency and on June 27, 1643 his estate was sequestered. [17]

CHITHURST

John de Wessilyr, rector of Chithurst, had a great dispute with Prior John of the small Priory of Pynham (see *Warningcamp*). The date was 1285, and the argument was all over an annual pension, payable half-yearly, arising from certain parish tithes. If the prior were not paid his instalments, the rector would be liable to a fine of one besant (a gold coin worth something less than £1). When the rector failed to pay up, the bishop of Chichester appointed an arbitrator who found in favour of the priory. The rector submitted, both parties went to the chapel at Midhurst and took solemn oaths to abide by the decision. A formal deed setting out the terms was drawn up and sealed by the bishop, and subscribed by eight or nine witnesses including a dean, an archdeacon and a parish priest. And the amount of the pension? Five shillings (25p.) a year. [8]

CHRIST'S HOSPITAL

In the chapel of the great school is a series of sixteen large murals by distinguished Sussex artist Frank Brangwyn, who lived for much of his life at Ditchling, and whose name is commemorated in Estates, Roads and Drives in several parts of Sussex. [3/10]

CHURCH NORTON

St. Wilfrid is recalled under *Selsey* in *Hidden Sussex*. He came to Sussex after quarrelling with Ecgfrith, lord of Northumbria, and found the Sussex people so backward that they couldn't even fish — an art which he taught them.   [25]

CLAPHAM

Michelgrove was one of the country's longest-established estates; it is recorded in the days of Henry III as belonging to the le Fauconer family. About 1314 they adopted the name of their home as their own surname, calling themselves de Michelgrove. Two centuries later the last representative of the family was a girl, Elizabeth, who married John Shelley; he died in 1526. The couple were progenitors of branches of the Shelleys who settled at Lewes, Patcham, Castle Goring and Penshurst, as well as continuing the Michelgrove line. The house itself, which Henry VIII had visited, was bought in 1828 by the then Duke of Norfolk, who completely demolished it.

The Shelley family included a judge, a Grand Prior of the Order of St. John of Jerusalem, a Knight of Rhodes killed during the defence of the island, and of course one of England's greatest poets. We noted in *Hidden Sussex* the existence of several Shelley memorials in Clapham church.[19]

CLAYTON

Where Clayton Priory now stands there was once a fine house called 'Hammond's Place'. It was built in 1566 by Edward Michelborne, and on his death it passed to his son Sir Edward. Edward was a participant in the Earl of Essex's rebellion but was pardoned by Queen Elizabeth. In 1604 he was granted a royal licence to explore and trade with China, Japan, Korea and other Far Eastern lands. You can read the details of his voyage in Lower's *Worthies of Sussex*, as well as Lower's comment that it was "difficult to attribute to Sir Edward Michelborne any creditable motive for this rash and unprofitable enterprise. It was more like piracy than honest trading."   [20]

CLIMPING

In 1524 Margaret Hartley (or Hartlee) made her will. Like several other testators in our book, she was punctilious over her bequests, including several to the church. She gave to the Rood-light a quarter of wheat, and to every light in the body of the church 'one bushell of whete'. One wonders why such distinction — a bushel would have been 8 gallons, a quarter eight times as much again. She also gave the church 'a cow for an obitt to be kept yerly, with dirge and masse for my soll'. And, most remarkable of all, she gave her wedding-ring to the Rood-Cross in the church.   [26]

COATES

The first Duke of Abercorn was created in 1868; he died in 1885. His widow was Louisa Jane, second daughter of the sixth Duke of Bedford. She was born in 1812 and died at Coates Castle in 1905, having lived there ever since the death of her husband. She was generous to the church, spending much money on its restoration early in this century, and a plaque recording her benevolence is to be found inside.   [9]

COCKING

Adam de Bavent, who died in 1292 must, despite his name, have been a true Englishman in defence of his rights. In 1279 he established by a legal action his right to 'free chase' on the manor land. The only condition was that the Earl of Arundel also had a personal right to hunt over the same land. Some years later Adam complained that the Earl had entered his free chase; but the jury found for the Earl. Adam also alleged, unsuccessfully, that the Earl had cut down some of his trees — perhaps the Earl's undoubted power in the area influenced the jury's decision. A couple of years after this, Adam tried again — this time against 'certain other hunters' — and was awarded damages. His genuine local concern is evidenced by his application in 1285, on behalf of the manor, for a weekly market and a three-day annual fair in Cocking. His request was granted, and both market and fair persisted for a long while.[17]

COKEHAM

Medieval people took quite seriously many things which now appear quaint, if not actually ridiculous. In 1262 Thomas de Brom settled the manor of Cokeham, near Worthing, and that of Stanham on Walter de la Hyde and his wife Joan. The rent was fixed as a pair of white gloves and a penny at Easter. In the following century the manor was given to the monks of Hardham Priory — no doubt the manorial revenues came in useful to a priory which was never wealthy: but records don't tell us any more about the white gloves.   [19]

COLDWALTHAM

In 1622 the churchwardens must have been uncommonly zealous, seeing the complaints they wrote in their 'presentments' for that year. The entertaining guide pamphlet for the church and village gives some extracts:-

'There is Roger Brookfield and Thomas Smyth, alehowskeepers, which due (do) keepe resort in the tyme of divine service.' Later, smarting under their victims' ripostes, they wrote, 'Also we present Thomas Smyth and Roger Brookfield for that they did give us the churchwardens evill speeches (because wee did present them) ...' But no target was beyond the reach of these dignitaries, because in the same year 'We present our minister because he doth not say prayers in due tyme; for sometymes we have noe prayer upon the Sabbath day ...'   [9]

COLEMAN'S HATCH

More than any other Sussex forest, Ashdown Forest has been the focus of legal disputes. A series in the 19th century culminated in a High Court case between Earl de la Warr, Lord of the Manor of Duddleswell, and Bernard Hale, a prominent local landowner and magistrate who upheld the Commoners' cause. Another champion of the Commoners was Judge Robert Melville, who lived at Hartfield Grove, Coleman's Hatch. A plaque erected by his family in Hartfield church says he was 'primarily responsible in 1882 for securing the Commoners' rights', though the Act of Parliament finally settling the dispute was passed only in 1885. Though the Earl retained the land of the Forest, rights of grazing, cutting bracken and so on were confirmed for the Commoners, and the public were given access to specified parts of the area.   [5]

COLWORTH

A common name in this part of Sussex is Peachey. But in the reign of Charles I and earlier it was spelt Peché, in the French manner. The family were lessees of this manor through the greater part of the seventeenth and eighteenth centuries.   [18]

COMPTON

At Little Green, north of the village on the Harting road, lived Sir Harold Reckitt, founder of the company which made Reckitt's Blue for laundries. His concern amalgamated with Colman's, who made starch — and the whole organisation now markets an enormous range of products including mustard. Sir Harold was patron of North Marden church.   [29]

COOKSBRIDGE

McBeans Orchids have been known in the village for over a century. James Ure McBean, a native of Dingwall in Northern Scotland, bought land here in 1875 and built his first greenhouse four years later. Now the firm is known worldwide for its endless new varieties and for the hundreds of prizes it has won. The other big orchid name in Sussex used to be Charlesworth & Co. of Haywards Heath, a business taken over by McBeans in 1971.   [21]

COOMBES

John Galsworthy, author of 'The Forsyte Saga' and other famous novels, was almost all his life a Sussex man. Although he died at Bury (see *Hidden Sussex*) he was born at Coombes in 1867. But far more was contributed to local prosperity by the Gell family. Francis Gell was a most enterprising farmer who reclaimed many acres of acid land by constructing a river wall in the 1790s. He introduced several new crops to the area including turnips, potatoes, sainfoin and clover, besides much augmenting the local population of sheep.   [20]

COOTHAM

The village hall here was originally a chapel, built in Victorian times at the instigation of Lord Zouche, because the nearest church was too far away for easy access, and services were needed for this little community. When travel became easier round about 1900, congregations declined, and in 1904 services were discontinued. In 1922 Lady Zouche agreed that the chapel should be turned to secular uses, and as the village hall it is still capable of providing a valuable local amenity.

Our researches have failed to show if Mr. Reeves here was the last of his kind in the county, but we do know that as recently as 1930 he used to tour the district as carrier with his horse and cart, blowing a horn to announce his arrival in places like Sullington and West Chiltington. [18]

COPTHORNE

In 1927 the Sussex County Magazine described otter hunting as 'a comparatively new sport'. Copthorne was its base and Sydney Varndell, Master of the Crowhurst Otter Hounds (they were owned by a Crowhurst woman but kennelled here) declared himself pleased 'that one has played one's part in providing healthy entertainment for one's fellows'. The magazine's account of the proceedings will, however, make unpleasant reading for today's conservationists:

> After an hour's hard work for the huntsman and his hounds the otter begins to tire and to show more often, coming to the surface of the water and sometimes landing in the dense undergrowth; then it is that hounds show their mettle and knowledge as they give him no peace, until one hound gets a hold and, the rest of the pack joining him, they kill the otter in mid-stream . [5]

COWBEECH

Samuel Dallaway, founder of the great family of East Sussex millers (see also *Punnett's Town* and *Stone Cross*) acquired the mill in 1839 when it was about twenty years old, and he worked it for almost forty years until his death in 1878. However, at Cowbeech the mill ceased to be wind-driven in 1860 when Samuel acquired a Cornish boiler and steam became the motive power. [23]

COWDRAY

Although Sir David Owen became tenant of Cowdray for life by marrying into the Bohun family, evidence exists that his son Henry purported to sell the property for £2,193 6s 8d while his father was still alive and therefore the rightful owner! The purchaser, who took over after Sir David's death in 1535, was Sir William Fitzwilliam, KG, Lord Keeper of the Privy Seal and Lord High Admiral. He was created Earl of Southampton in 1537 and remains one of our most distinguished residents at any time. [8]

COWFOLD

The mystery of Prior Thomas Nelond's famous brass (see *Hidden Sussex*) is why it should be here. What we have discovered is that he was the 26th prior of St Pancras at Lewes, who presided over that institution's fortunes from 1421-1429 and died in 1432. Was the brass always here, or was it brought from somewhere else? [11]

CRIPPS CORNER

Local legend has it that Cripps was a highwayman, but (alas for legend!) the truth is that in the 15th century the area belonged to one John Cryps, who's mentioned in a document dated 1432. Early in the present century a wheelwright named Tedham lived here. He was also the village undertaker, but his speciality was making the big Sussex farm waggons, and one of them (with his trade plate on it) can be seen at Michelham Priory. [15]

CROSS-IN-HAND

It may seem a strange name for a village, but it perpetuates a glorious part of history. It was the local rallying-point for our forefathers at the time when they were starting off for the Crusades. As they made away on their long journey each would hold a Cross in his hand. Seek no further for the name. [13]

CROWBOROUGH

Sherlock Holmes' creator Sir Arthur Conan Doyle lived at Windlesham Manor from 1906 until his death in 1930, and people like Kipling, G. B. Shaw and the famous barrister Marshall Hall were regular visitors. He arrived in Crowborough already famous and knighted: he had intended to refuse the honour and was persuaded by his mother, but he salved his conscience by having Holmes offered a 'K' on the very same day (in *The Three Garridebs*) and turning it down! Although he wrote Sherlock Holmes stories here, the only book to have Windlesham Manor for its setting was *The Poison Belt*, one of his science fiction novels featuring Professor Challenger. Conan Doyle was buried in the grounds but his remains were later moved to a grave in the New Forest. [6]

CROWHAM

Payment in kind: in 1211-1212 Hugh de Peplesham held land at Crowham by the service of finding a ship for the 'passage of the Count and Countess' (presumably of Eu) and for this service he was given a robe. The records don't show how often this event was due to take place. [**24**

CROWHURST

There's nothing remarkable about the iron graveslab at Crowhurst which records, in quaint English, the resting place of Anne Forster. But

it's very strange that copies of this slab can be found all over Sussex used as firebacks. Was there a plan to establish that Anne was, indeed, Thomas Gainsford's heir? A less cynical explanation is that the local ironfounder re-used the one mould for the sake of economy.

There are some ardent Puritan names in the 17th century church registers: Obedience Fuller, Repentance Gascoigne, Temperance Bramford and Freegift and Bethankfull Gower. The last was male, the others female, though as far as we know there is no clue in the names themselves.

'The King of Letter-Writers' was rector here from 1889 until 1917. The Rev. James Price Bacon-Phillips (1857-1938) claimed that between 8,000 and 9,000 of his letters to the Press had been seen in print, adding that there were thousands more whose fate he had been unable to check. He wrote his first in 1879 but really got going in 1892 when his pet hobby-horse was the way in which witnesses in the courts were bullied by opposing counsel. 'I have strongly defended,' he said, 'little children, tramps, the aged poor, cabmen, busmen and animals, particularly horses.' [**24**]

CROWLINK

The gangleader Jevington Jig shamelessly ran with the hare and hunted with the hounds. In 1792 he was officially acting as assistant to the revenue officers — no better than a supergrass. In March he was arrested for horse-stealing while in the service of H.M. Customs. The horse in question had belonged to Jig's own gang and he had helped the law officers to seize it — after which he tried to make off on the very same horse!

E. Nesbit, author of *The Railway Children*, lived here for a time.[**28**]

CUCKFIELD

What's in a name? When Charles Sergison, one of the controllers of William III's Navy, bought the manor of Cuckfield in 1691 he determined that his considerable estate should be passed on to Sergisons even though he was himself childless and the last bearer of the family name. His idea was that whoever was next in line to inherit should do so only if he took the Sergison name — a practice which continued into the 20th century. There were bitter legal disputes among rival would-be beneficiaries within a few decades of his death in 1732, but the most sensational court case was heard at the Guildhall in London in July 1820. It revolved around this question: was 14-year-old Harriet Sergison the daughter of the (deceased) Col. Francis Sergison and his wife or of 'a common prostitute living in the city of Dublin'? Unhappily for Harriet, she was found to be the latter, and so lost everything. The colonel's wife, it transpired, had paid three crowns for the baby just after it had been delivered to 18-year-old Ann Higgins in an ale house. We're indebted to local historian Maisie Wright for her research into this story, which suggests that Harriet was none too convincingly represented by the Solicitor General. How had Col. Sergison slept nightly with his wife and not noticed that she was pregnant? 'He seems to have been very much addicted to drinking,' observed this worthy, 'and such a person does not very often go to bed quite in that state of mind as to be capable of making observations'!

The other historic local family are the Burrells, who made a fortune in the late Middle Ages as ironmasters before coming to Cuckfield. In 1483 Gerard Burrell, vicar of Cuckfield, bought Ockenden House (now known as Ockenden Manor), which the family still owns. His descendants followed a variety of occupations, but always with distinction. Ninian Burrell, who died in 1628 at the early age of 27, was a lawyer; Counsellor Timothy Burrell was born in 1643 and duly called to the Bar, until in 1683 he succeeded to the family estate, over which he presided until his death; and Percy Burrell was killed in 1807 while a serving soldier in South America.

Timothy Burrell from the time he took over the estates kept a diary which is filled with amusing little sketches and wry entries, such as 'Paid John Coachman for a whip to spoil my horses, 1s. 6d.' and (in reference to a workman paling an orchard fence) 'worked three days but gently'.

We illustrate a charming statuette over the door of the old smith's house. [11]

DALLINGTON

In medieval times running feuds between churches and neighbouring monks seem to have been quite common. In 1473 the Prior of Warbleton laid a formal complaint against the vicar of Dallington, Thomas Greene, accusing him (among much else) of appropriating two gold cups and of using the priory seal on various leases — presumably to pocket the rents. Then, as now, the best form of defence was attack: the vicar replied that the cups had been left with him as security for a loan he'd made to the previous prior. As for the seal, that was in the prior's own custody and the prior should know all about it.

It was only in 1938 that Alfred Edwin Tutton died here, yet the inexorable spread of the metric system already gives his achievement an archaic ring. It was by his methods that the length of the Imperial Yard was officially determined. **[14]**

DANEHILL

The barrister Thomas Henry Davies (Advocate-General to the East India Company in Calcutta from around 1785 until 1791) left a large estate to his widow and three sons, two of whom bought up most of what is now Danehill. The elder, named Warburton, took the northern half, the younger, Francis, the southern, including the area where the house called Danehurst lies. Danehurst was bought in the 1870s by Herbert Carey Hardy who married Adela Knight, Jane Austen's niece. Hardy, the local squire, died from shock in 1888 after having his leg amputated because of a carriage accident. He was just 40.

Margery Corbett, an early leader of the women's rights movement, was born here in 1882. The family lived at a house which used to be called Woodgate, but later became known as Cumnor House: it's now a boys' school. She became interested in politics when young, and by the age of 19, in 1902, was national secretary of the Constitutional Suffrage Movement. In 1924 she was elected president of the International Alliance of Women, but she made her greatest mark as one of the UK delegates to the ill-starred disarmament conference at Geneva in 1932. In 1910 she married Brian Ashby, but she retained the use of her maiden name and was always known as Dame Margery Corbett Ashby. At the age of 90 she became first president of the Danehill Parish Historical Society, to whom she talked vividly for a full 80 minutes five years later. When she died in 1981, almost a centenarian, the society published a commemorative book on her life which makes fascinating reading. **[12]**

DENTON

Diones Geere, the curate here in 1793, took an advertisement in the local press to complain that his rector owed him arrears of salary. The rector lived in London and, though he had a good income, was constrained to change his address frequently, for reasons which may be guessed at. The Rev. Geere, naming the rector and giving the figure owed, expressed the hope that no other clergyman would be so unbrotherly as to accept the job until he himself was paid. **[27]**

DIAL POST

Alongside the A24 stands a gaunt ruin, the sole remains of Knepp Castle, once owned by the de Braoses (see *Introduction*). King John stayed here at least twice although no love was lost between the Braoses and the king. In 1199 John had been nominated king since Prince Arthur of Brittany, intended as successor to king Richard I on the throne of England, was a mere boy. John bestowed on William de Braose large areas of land in Wales and elsewhere. But in 1203 the prince, only 16, was brutally murdered in France. William knew the secret of Arthur's murder and was unwise enough not to keep his mouth shut. John heard about William's indiscretions; he seized all the de Braose estates, including Knepp, and drove William into exile. Then he grabbed William's wife and heir, imprisoned them in Windsor Castle and callously starved them to death.

A couple of centuries passed, and more peaceful times came. In 1399 William Roger was appointed park-keeper of 'Knap' for life, with the fees and profits and twopence a day out of the issue of the manor. Apparently at the time Knepp was in the hands of the Mowbrays, so one would like to know what the 'fees and profits' could have been.   **[10]**

DIDLING

A local resident in this remote hamlet, and member of the church congregation, was Anthony Armstrong Willis, the author of many contributions to *Punch* and other magazines over the initials 'A.A.'.   **[8]**

DITCHLING

It would be impossible to find space for a mention of all the famous names associated with Ditchling. They range from artists like Eric Gill and Frank Brangwyn (see *Christ's Hospital*) through the poetess Mrs. Meynell, to the actress Ellen Terry and, in our own times, Dame Vera Lynn and cartoonist Rowland Emmett. So we read through Henry Cheal's book on the village and selected John Burgess, a businessman of two centuries ago, who kept a diary from 1785 to 1815. He called it a 'Jernel', and his readiness to write was in no way hampered by his inability to spell. He seems to have been village Jack-of-all-trades, being tailor, glover (he had to get a licence for this), bellows-mender, carpenter, preacher, gravedigger and many more things. On January 19, 1786, he 'went to Keymer with several people in pursuit of the person soposed to have robbed Mrs. Brown's shop, it was soposed he was concealed in old Mooryes House and by virtue of a warrant we serched his house but did not find the man but found several things soposed to have been stollen ...' A man named Fox was eventually tried for the offence at Horsham Assizes and hanged.   **[20]**

DONNINGTON

The Victorians obliterated so many medieval wall paintings that it's surprising to learn that the vicar here in 1875, a man named Stansfield, executed his own version of the Crucifixion above the chancel arch. His parishioners for some reason disapproved of it, however, and it was boarded over for a number of years. [25]

DRAGONS GREEN

We know of no other place where you can find a tombstone outside a pub, and there's a poignant tale behind this curiosity. Walter Budd, an albino and an epileptic, drowned himself days after his 26th birthday in 1893 after being accused of a trivial theft. Walter, who was evidently the butt of unkindness by the local children, had lived with his parents at the George and Dragon. The monument they erected over his grave in Shipley churchyard carried the words: 'May God forgive those who forgot their duty to him who was just and afflicted.' This was too much for the vicar and some of the locals to take and the Budds were asked to remove the stone. It still stands where they defiantly placed it, by the road in front of their pub.

On the right hand side of the minor road towards Brooks Green, just before a fairly sharp right hand bend, is the sturdily constructed head of what's known as Abraham's Well. We're told that the little spring never dries up even during times of drought, but who Abraham was, and why he built his well so far from the local hamlets, we have no idea. [10]

DRAYTON

An ancient manor belonging to Boxgrove Priory at least since the time of Edward III, Drayton passed to the Chatfield family after the Dissolution in 1536. George Chatfield was mayor of Chichester in 1586 at a time when the office was far more active and far less of a figurehead than it is today. Later the manor came to the Elson family, which from 1662 provided the county with at least one High Sheriff and three members of Parliament in the space of 60 years. [17]

DUDDLESWELL

Edward III and his son John of Gaunt loved to hunt on Ashdown Forest. About a mile or so north of the hamlet, just off the B2188, is a place still known as King's Standing. It's on a hill and was almost certainly an observation point where the royal party stopped to reconnoitre.   [12]

DUNCTON

Two notable all-round cricketers were born here. James Broadbridge, born in 1796, was evidently a man of great stamina and would walk as far as Brighton (nearly 30 miles away) in order to play. James Dean, born in 1816, was known variously as Joyous Jemmy, Dean Swift and The Sussex Ploughboy. John Wisden, of the invaluable Guide, was one of the friends staying with him over Christmas 1881 at the Cricketers Arms, which he kept in his later years. On Christmas morning they woke to find that Dean had died in his sleep. He was buried in the old Duncton churchyard. But whose portrait graces the sign outside the pub? Logic would seem to suggest that it's Dean's, but we've heard claims for both Dean and Broadbridge.

In the new churchyard is the grave of Florence de Fonblanque, leader of the Women's Suffrage march from Edinburgh to London in 1912, who died in 1949 having seen the implementation of most of the reforms she fought for.
                                    [9]

DURFORD ABBEY

This is the smallest abbey we've come across, with only two acres of land near the river Rother west of Rogate. At the suppression of the monasteries Sir Edmund Mervyn was sent to inquire into allegations of embezzlement by the abbot. Sir Edmund, a Justice of the King's Bench, did well out of the affair: he was granted the abbey site.   [29]

DURRINGTON

The case of the venal churchwarden. In the late 1670s, while the church was being restored after Civil War depredations, the chapel bell went missing. The overseers were summoned before the consistory court of the diocese and said they had heard reports 'that the bell was sold for about foure or five pounds and carried to Sir Charles Shellyes at Mitchellgrove within the parish of Clapham by one Thomas Caplin'. The curate, Richard Pawley, had another story, averring that Robert Collins of Durrington had sold it to Goodman Green of Tarring. Collins duly came before the court and admitted that he and Caplin, a churchwarden, had sold the bell 'and laid out the same money towards the relief of the poor'. Whatever the truth of this last claim, Caplin was ordered either to pay the money into court or get the bell back and take it to Mr Pawley.   [19]

EARNLEY

The mill offers one of those stories of long-established family businesses which are scattered throughout our book. Somerley Mill, as it was sometimes known, was bought by the Stevens brothers in 1845 and was owned by the family for all of 97 years. The miller during the second world war was a Mr Ellis. When he retired in 1942 it was taken over by the Bartholomews of Chichester. [25]

EARTHAM

William Hayley the poet lived at Eartham House from 1774-1800. He entertained many of the artistic élite of his day, including the painter Romney, the historian Edward Gibbon (see *Fletching*) and the poet Cowper. His son Thomas was a sculptor, a pupil of the great John Flaxman who carved the monument on the west wall at the north side of the church nave. In 1800 Hayley sold the house to William Huskisson, a great financial expert who became MP for the city of Chichester, holding the seat from 1812-1823 — stirring years! On September 15, 1830, Huskisson was attending the opening of the Liverpool and Manchester Railway when he was struck by Stephenson's Rocket, dying within a few hours — the first ever victim of a railway accident. [17/18]

EASEBOURNE

The waywardness of the nuns of Easebourne Priory is part of local folklore. In 1441 the sisterhood was in financial difficulty and the nuns complained to the bishop of Chichester that the Prioress made them work too hard while she appropriated any income they might earn. They also said that she spent money recklessly, often taking an unnecessarily large retinue on her frequent travels from the priory, and that she was too fond of delicate food and fancy clothing: the trimmings of her mantle were said to be worth a hundred shillings! Things went from bad to worse. There was a scandal that the Prioress had given birth to at least one child, while two other nuns had absconded — they, too, having increased the population statistics. The internal administration of the priory was beset by squabbles and, in this case at least, the Dissolution in 1535 was probably no bad thing.

The curate here in 1851 was Canon Ellerton, one of the country's most prolific hymn writers. Among his works was 'The day Thou gavest, Lord, is ended'. [8]

EAST BLATCHINGTON

John Brocas, lord of the manor here in 1377, was among a group of people, including the Prior of Lewes, taken prisoner while trying to repel French raiders who had landed at Rottingdean. In his absence his cousin Sir Edmund Fitzherbert took possession, and through his sister Alice the manor later came into the hands of the Lords de la Warr. (See *Introduction*, page 10).

John Willett was one of those many people who displeased the church authorities. In 1628 his 'irreverend behaviour in the church' was brought to the notice of the Archdeaconry Court of Lewes: '. . . sitting with his hat on his head in tyme of divine service . . . throwing stones at others that set in the chancell in tyme of divine service and sermon to the disturbing of the minister and the rest of the congregation . . . fighting in the churchyard and . . . a very negligent comer to the Church on the Sabbath day.'   [20].

EAST CHILTINGTON

Susannah Stacey was the heroine of Marcus Woodward's *The Mistress of Stantons Farm*. At a time when belladonna was in great demand for poultices she cultivated it in Cripps' Plantation at the foot of the Downs. Eventually there were ample supplies from abroad and the plantation was allowed to run wild, but when there was a sudden demand in the first world war the plants were found to be still abundant and large quantities were harvested. Susannah Stacey is buried in Westmeston churchyard.

How many humble men and women in days gone by might have achieved great things had they had the opportunity? James Nye, born in East Chiltington in 1822, was a self-educated poet, musician, composer and instrument-maker (his violin is in the Anne of Cleves House museum at Lewes), who worked as an agricultural labourer, quarryman and gardener. Queenspark Publications in Brighton recently published his short autobiography, edited by Vic Gammon *(A small account of my travels through the wilderness)*. For Protestants there was always a tension between the spirituality and the sensuality of church music and Nye, himself a Calvinist, agonizes over it:

I was so fond of music that I
made a complete idol of it, and
I am not quite clear of this
idolatry now I am writing
these lines, for there is something in music and singing
which touches so clean on my
natural part that I cannot help
being carried away with the
sound instead of the substance. [21]

EAST DEAN (East Sussex)

Parson Jonathan Darby was vicar here from 1715-1728. At Belle Tout cliff he hollowed out a staircase and a cavern as a means of escape for shipwrecked sailors, of whom there were many in this area. He would shine a light from one of the caverns, since called 'Parson Darby's Hole', out to sea — coast erosion caused it to vanish a century or more ago. But the tongue of scandal will always wag, and cynics said that he liked to go there to escape from a nagging wife. The lighthouse at Belle Tout was erected in 1831, but was found to get fogbound very readily, so the light at Beachy Head replaced it. (See *Birling*).

A rather eerie story concerns two sisters, Agnes and Joan (or Johan) Payne. Agnes, the elder, was taken ill, and lay bereft of speech and evidently near death. Suddenly, after lying still and silent for over 24 hours, she called to her sister to make herself ready and come with her. Joan, who was in good health and busy around the house, was sent for. When she asked Agnes how she was, Agnes again bade her make ready; she was waiting for her and could not go alone. Within half an hour Joan was taken ill, growing worse overnight, while again and again Agnes called for her. 'In the morninge', we read in the church register, 'they both departed this wretched world together.' The story's accuracy was vouched for by the vicar and the two churchwardens. [28]

EAST DEAN (West Sussex)

Somewhere, space must be found for William Cobbett, author of *Rural Rides*. He was not a Sussex man, but he spent much time riding through our county, noting what he saw, and supplying for posterity a fascinating record of fact, near-fact and often bilious comment. But he was much on the side of the countryman. "I called to me a young man," he wrote of a trip at East Dean, "who, along with other turnip-hoers, was sitting under the shelter of a hedge at breakfast. I was glad to see that his food consisted of a good lump of household bread and not a very small piece of bacon. In parting with him, I said, 'You do get some bacon, then?' 'Oh, yes, sir', said he, and with an emphasis and with a swag of the head which seemed to say, 'We *must* and *will* have that!'" [17]

EASTERGATE

In the parish church is an oddity — a memorial window to someone with no local connections. All the same .... at the house Northfield lived Mr. Edward Brandon. He was the brother-in-law of the personal secretary to Lord Kitchener of Khartoum. He conceived a great admiration for the General and gave to the church the east window as a Kitchener memorial. It was erected before the end of the 1914-18 War, as soon as possible after Kitchener's death. [18]

EAST GULDEFORD

A pilgrimage and a pomegranate feature in the story of the Guldeford family! It's not easy to find out whether Sir Richard Guldeford was named from this lonely district or whether he gave the family name to it. Either way, this isolated hamlet stands on the last part of Romney Marsh to be reclaimed from the sea. For ages uncounted it had been a region of grass tussocks swept by sea winds and often saturated at high tide. In 1480 Sir Richard rented some 1500 acres from Robertsbridge Abbey and built the sea wall which still protects the parish lands today. He drained the area with a network of 'cuttings' to make the Guldeford Saltings some of the best meat-producing land in the county and then built the brick church (consecrated in 1505) to mark the completion of his work on the 'innings'. After all this labour Sir Richard embarked at Rye to fulfil his life's ambition of making a devout pilgrimage to the Holy Land.

And the pomegranate? In 1519 Sir Henry Guldeford fought for King Ferdinand of Spain against the Moors. He was knighted at Burgos and granted the pomegranate as an augmentation of honour in the family's coat of arms. [16]

EASTHAMPNETT

Never more than a tiny place, it was classed as a 'tything' in the Middle Ages — that is, a group of ten houses or a tenth of the rural unit known as a 'hundred'. About 1674 the tything belonged to Sir George Jeffreys, who in a few years' time was to become the Lord Chancellor of England. [17]

EAST HOATHLY

One Sunday morning in the 1630s Colonel Thomas Lunsford, described as a wild friend of Charles Stuart, attempted to shoot his kinsman Sir Thomas Pelham outside East Hoathly church. Perhaps because he missed his target, this act of desecration led only to the severe fine of £8,000 by the Star Chamber, upon which he fled to France. The bullet hit the stonework on the south side of the west door of the church, where its trail can still be seen, then embedded itself in the solid oak of the door (remaining there for many years until eventually the door was replaced). In 1639 he returned to England, became reconciled with his cousin, obtained the King's pardon for his fines and was once more given command of a regiment.

We gave the celebrated diarist Thomas Turner a good mention in *Hidden Sussex*. Another, and more recent, noteworthy inhabitant of the district was the musician Ronald Binge. He lived at Barham House. [22]

EAST PRESTON

Elizabeth Corney kept a beer shop here in 1830, while James Booker was the village smith. Incredibly, in those days this now thriving retirement area comprised scarcely two dozen houses, with a short row of coastguard cottages almost on the shore. James and Elizabeth found themselves giving evidence in a trial whose after effects are still visible. The manor of Kingston was owned by George Olliver, and in 1830 a labourer in his employ named Edmund Bushby burnt down one of Olliver's hayricks. Bushby was found guilty, and was hanged on New Year's Day, 1831. Olliver received £500 reward for informing the authorities, and he used it to build and endow the Sunday School in 1840. At first it was but a single room, but it was enlarged over the years, and in its present state it's a bank and office in Sea Road.   [26]

EBERNOE

King Henry VIII's incessant need of finance was not satisfied when he seized the monasteries and their lands in the 1530s. By 1542 he was seeking other desirable properties — desirable, that is, for their sale or rental value. The manor of Ebernoe had been for centuries attached to the Honour of Arundel, but Henry took it as part of a large 'forcible exchange' with William, Earl of Arundel. The Crown retained it until 1592, and then it passed to a Mr. John Brown. He three years later sold it to one Mr John Smith (or Smyth). At least, this is the most likely line of descent, though alternative ones have been suggested; but how unexpected is the appearance of two such ordinary names.   [9]

EDBURTON

Tradition has it that the church pulpit and communion rails were the personal gift of the great Archbishop Laud (1573-1645). There seems no special reason when he should have donated them except that he probably preached here a few times, and that the archbishops of Canterbury have always been patrons of the living.

A rather unexpected visitor here was Oliver Wendell Holmes, the American author of *The Autocrat of the Breakfast Table* and other books. He called Edburton 'the nearest approach to Arcady one could hope to find.' Its then (1886) rector was, he said, a perfect replica of Goldsmith's parson in *The Deserted Village*.   [20]

EGDEAN

In 1663 George Bradshaw became resident minister here. His 'High Church' views had brought him into conflict with the Puritan faction during his previous living, in Berkshire. He was so hounded by the authorities that he spent one whole summer in the company of a charcoal-burner in Kent. Then he kept a small alehouse on the London to Portsmouth road near Cobham, in Surrey, to keep himself from starvation. After all that, and even on a salary of £30 a year, Egdean must have seemed a very heaven of peace.   [9]

ELSTED

What would our ancestors in the Middle Ages have given for a simple method of proving title to land! In the 13th century much of the land hereabouts belonged to the Gatesden family. When John de Gatesden died in 1258 he left his estate to his granddaughter Margaret, who married Sir John Camoys of nearby *Trotton.* This Sir John granted a lease of Elsted Manor to Henry Husee, but Husee died in 1290 with nine years of the lease still to run. Sir John resumed possession of the manor, but not for long! Sir William Paynel, whose title came directly from the Gatesdens and who held all the family's other estates, moved into Elsted Manor, forcibly chasing away the Camoys servants. Again, not for long! He, too, was evicted by the official Escheator, claiming in the name of the King. This sort of wrangle was all too common: within half a century Sir John's son, Sir Ralph, was himself the victim of a dispute of ownership between the Prior of Boxgrove and the Bishop of Exeter, both of whom claimed land dues from him.   [8]

ERIDGE

A branch of the Yorkshire family of Micklethwaite lived at Eridge Place, and there's a pleasing story of how Mr. Peckham Micklethwaite was created a baronet for coming to the rescue of the future Queen Victoria. It was on November 4, 1834, that the Princess was being taken by the Duchess of Kent to St Leonards-on-Sea in a landau. One of the two horses became entangled in its traces and fell, bringing the other down with it. As they lay thrashing on the ground, to the horror of the ladies, two passers-by ignored their own safety and sat on the first horse's head while the traces were cut. One of these men was Peckham Micklethwaite, and when Victoria became Queen she gave him his honour.   [6]

ETCHINGHAM

Sir William de Echyngham was responsible for the building of what's generally acknowledged to be the finest 14th century church in Sussex. He started work about 1360 and it must have been virtually completed by 1389, because on January 18 that year William died and a fine (though now mutilated) brass to him was laid in the chancel floor. It was the first of many family monuments in the church, until 1552 when Elizabeth de Echyngham married Sir Robert Tyrwhitt and the old name disappeared for ever. But the Echynghams had been known here since at least 1234, in which year Simon de Echyngham was Sheriff of Sussex and Surrey — an office he held for at least three years. The manor seems to have remained in the same family until the time of Elizabeth I.   [15]

EWHURST GREEN

Richard Weekes, descended from an old family of ironworkers, was an army officer during the disastrous war of 1689-97, in which Britain, Holland, France, Spain, Austria, Prussia and Hanover were all involved. In 1696 he wrote to his grandfather from Bensdorf, 'I and two of my Serjeants are here prisoners, taken upon suspicion. I have shew'd my commission, beating orders and warrant to take up desarters, but it would not prevaile. Therefore I shall desire you to speake to Sir John Newton, or ye Captain, to write ye leaste word imaginable to Justice Lide, to satisfie him that I am such a person and Ensign to such a Regiment, for otherwise I shall be forced to stay here or sent to prison ....'

From a later age comes the story of Rev. John Richardson, curate here for a bare three years. When John Wesley was preaching in the area, young Richardson, after attending to his own services, used to go off to listen to the great man. The Anglican parishioners complained and Rev. Richardson was dismissed. Wesley, always keen to enlist men in Holy Orders, took on Richardson and sent him to a meeting house in Moorfields. A century later the local Methodists paid the bulk of the cost of having electric light installed in the parish church as a memorial to Richardson — in those days such a display of community spirit between the two denominations must have been rare if not unique. [15]

EXCEAT

In 1891 the Rev. G. W. A. Lawrance, MA, was appointed rector of West Dean, near Seaford. Like many of 'the cloth', he was interested in history and antiquity, and in 1913 led the work of excavating the vanished village of Exceat. We must quote in full the inscription on the stone marking the site:-

> Here formerly stood the Parish Church of Excete, built probably in the XIth. century and abandoned in the XVth. century the parish being incorporated with West Dene in 1528. The foundations were uncovered under the supervision of the Revd. G. W. A. Lawrance, Rector of West Dene, and the Sussex Archaeological Society and the site reserved by the Ecclesiastical Commissioners 1913.

Round the side, incidentally, is another record of a man of Sussex: the monument bears the signature 'Andrews. Mason. Eastbourne.' [28]

FAIRLIGHT

"Owling" is a word long out of use. It meant smuggling in reverse — illegal exporting rather than importing — and it was highly lucrative, unless one got caught. In the eighteenth century a Protectionist policy forbade the export of sheep or wool, and owlers there were a-plenty. In 1787 Thomas Harman of Fairlight was tried for exporting wool out of the kingdom, and was fined three shillings for every pound weight exported — a total, in his case, of the then colossal sum of £732. Then John Harman was tried at Westminster for exporting not merely wool but whole sheep, and he was fined £3,899 4s. Penalties of this size, one would think, must have acted as a powerful deterrent, but owling went on until the law was repealed.

A local musical celebrity was Dr Thomas A. Walmisley (1814-1856), friend of Mendelssohn and composer of anthems still beloved of church choirs. Settings by him of the Magnificat and Nunc Dimittis have been recorded several times. He became Professor of Music at Cambridge at the age of 22, and revered Bach. [24]

FAIRWARP

On the night of July 31, 1941, a Wellington bomber returning from a raid on Cologne crashed near here, on the edge of Ashdown Forest. The mother of Sgt. Pilot Victor Ronald Sutton erected a memorial which has now been given a wall of local stone. Although it is commonly called 'the airmen's grave', no one is actually buried there. An inscription reads, 'To the glorious memory of Sgt./P.V.R. Sutton, aged 24 years, 142 Bom. Sqdn. R.A.F, also his five comrades who lost their lives through enemy action. 31-7-41. Mother.' Standing alone on a path in the forest, it's best reached from Hollies car park. [12]

FALMER

A magic name in journalism in the 1930s and 1940s was that of Godfrey Winn. He had a regular column in 'The Daily Mirror' for years, particularly appealing to women. His home was at Falmer for a long time. [21]

FAYGATE

In 1524 the owner of Beaubush, now spelt Bewbush, the principal estate here, was Sir Thomas Seymour, Lord Sudeley, brother of the Protector Somerset, and himself a man of no mean ambition. He had married Queen Catherine Parr, widow of Henry VIII, and at her death ("not without suspicion of poison", wrote Burnet in his *History*), he ardently courted Queen Elizabeth I. As he was Lord High Admiral and a favourite in royal circles, his attentions were tolerated for a time. Then the scheme was found out, and he was sent to the Tower and condemned to execution without being allowed any defence. [4]

FELPHAM

William Blake's span at Felpham was a matter of only about three years, but for two reasons it cannot be ignored. First, the importance of Blake as artist and poet, and second, his own feelings about his 'slumber on the banks of ocean.' He called Felpham 'the sweetest spot on earth' soon after his arrival in 1800 when he was forty-three. He came to Felpham at the invitation of William Hayley (see *Eartham*), to whom he had been introduced by the sculptor Flaxman. Close to Hayley's home in the village was a small cottage which he lent to the fiery genius. And here was the setting for a most bizarre episode.

In 1803, without telling Blake, his gardener asked a soldier whom he knew to do some work in the garden. So when Blake found a stranger on his premises, he politely asked him to leave. The soldier's impudent reply goaded Blake into a temper and he frogmarched the soldier down the lane. The latter, bent on revenge, concocted a story that Blake had said words like, "Damn the king, damn his soldiers", and "When Bonaparte comes, I'll help him." Blake was accused of sedition and treason, brought before Quarter Sessions at Chichester — and predictably acquitted, amid scenes of jubilant uproar in the courtroom. [26]

FERNHURST

Few people in England can have researched their village history more thoroughly or more lovingly than did Alice M. Tudor, whose *Fernhurst* was published in 1934 and reissued in 1969. Her labours brought to light the sad story of Jone (Joan) Mellishe, who made her will in 1587 when only 25. She gave 4d to the cathedral at Chichester and 8d. to her parish church. She gave her personal belongings around her family with a nice sense of propriety. One of her god-daughters had 'my worser pinne of silver', her sister Alice had 'my best hat, my best nickersher' (i.e. neckerchief) 'saving one, one double kercher with two pieces of linen called skwares', and her sister-in-law 'one of my rails' (a part of her underwear) 'next unto the best'. At the time she was in bed with what seems to have been a severe chill which looked like proving fatal, and village gossips were blaming it on the horseplay of a local lad named Foke Oklle (perhaps Ockley). So Jone tried to get him off the hook by writing in her will, 'Whereas it has been thought by some and also reported that my sickness and visitacion should com by the meanes and negligence of one Foke Oklle who at a sheepe washe tokin and set me into the water wherefore this is to make it knowne unto all men that I do neyther so thinke nor yet am so persuaded but that my visitacion is onely by the visitacion of almightie god and not otherwise, and as touching the said foke oklle I do here in my said sickness with all my hart freely forgive him as I would myself be forgiven at the Handes of God.' [1]

FERRING

One of the English saints lived for a time at Ferring, and in straitened circumstances, too. He was Richard de Wyche, who was elected Bishop of Chichester in 1244 but was effectively dispossessed of his living by Henry III. Few people dared to help him but the priest of Ferring took him in and Richard stayed for two years, ministering to the poor in their hovels until the King gave way. He's said to have worked miracles in his lifetime and was canonised as Saint Richard in 1262.

John Moore, who died in February 1895 aged 90, was a shoemaker who in his youth had been very active in the smuggling industry. Respectability intervened, however, and in 1894 he celebrated his 70th wedding anniversary. Queen Victoria sent him a message of congratulation — and a gift of three pounds. [26]

FINDON

William Frankland introduced a wide range of machinery to Muntham Manor. Born in 1720 in Bengal, he later travelled to Europe via the deserts of the Middle East — and he apparently chose Findon for his retirement because the Downs in some way reminded him of those landscapes! He installed lathes, clocks, printing machines, spinning, weaving and tailoring equipment and an unusual horizontal windmill to raise water for the house. [19]

FIRLE

Penelope Darcy was a 17th century beauty who had three lovers at once. They used to quarrel over her, but she silenced them by promising that if they would be patient she would marry them all in turn. So she did: her first husband was Sir George Trenchard, her second Sir John Gage, her third Sir William Hervey.

The most colourful of the Gage family, who have lived at Firle Place for centuries, was undoubtedly Joseph, younger of the two grandsons of the second baronet. He invested heavily in France in the scheme for developing the Mississippi and made a vast paper fortune. Entertaining fantastic dreams of becoming eminent, he offered to pay the King of Poland £3 million for his crown. On receiving a refusal, he made a similar offer for the throne of Sardinia: this, too, was rejected. When the bubble of his financial scheme burst he went off to Spain, ingratiated himself with authority, and was soon granted a royal patent for working all the gold mines in Old Spain and fishing for wrecks off the coast. In 1741 the Spanish king presented him with a valuable silver mine and the title of Count. Between 1743 and 1746 he was commander-in-chief of the Spanish army in Italy against the Austrians, and was given a pension of 4,000 ducats a year (a handsome sum) by the King of Naples. After this he seems to have quietened down somewhat. [21]

FISHBOURNE

It would be wrong to regard the Roman invasion of Britain as a bad thing for all concerned — and the native king Tiberius Claudius Cogidubnus (as he later liked to be known) certainly found it highly advantageous. With his tribe under pressure from its neighbours, Cogidubnus apparently offered Rome the mastery of Sussex — a useful base for later conquests — in return for his people's protection and his own advancement. He was appointed a legate for his services, which meant that he was actually entitled to sit in the senate in Rome. The sumptuous palace unearthed at Fishbourne was almost certainly his. [17]

FISHERSTREET

How was it that during the 1950s a peer, Earl Winterton, was Father of the House of Commmons? The answer is that he was a peer of Ireland and so not debarred from election to Parliament as a commoner! The Earls had lived at Shillinglee Park from the late 18th century until the mansion was largely burnt out during the second world war. [2]

FITTLEWORTH

When the Rev. Henry Latham died in 1859 his widow lived on in the village and spent much of her time researching local superstitions. In 1868 she published a fascinating pamphlet about them. For example, it was considered an infallible cure for whooping cough to take whatever remedy was prescribed by the rider of a piebald horse! It's on record that a man in Petworth who used to ride such a horse was often accosted by an anxious mother seeking a remedy, and whatever the rider suggested seemed to work. As a cure for rupture in a child he was to be attended by nine persons who should pass him nine times a day for nine days through a cleft made by an axe in a sound ash sapling.

Canon Arthur Barwick Simpson was a pioneer in the tuning of church bells. When rector at Fittleworth during the last quarter of the 19th century he published an account of his researches into the subject. Although a bell might seem to sound only one note, what you hear is actually a mixture of tones. Simpson's 'five tone principle' argued that bells should be tuned more scientifically one with another, and his methods have been followed in this country ever since.

The English composer Edward Elgar (1857-1934) lived at Brinkwells for a time, and it was here that he composed his great Cello Concerto and his best-known chamber music. Alice Elgar described the autumnal mood she sensed in her husband's music while they lived in Sussex as 'wood magic'. [9]

FIVE ASHES

'Twitts Ghyll' lies down a deep rutted lane, as secluded a spot as anyone could desire. One who did desire it was Sir Austen Chamberlain, son of the great Joseph and a fine parliamentarian himself. He was Chancellor of the Exchequer in 1903, a loyal supporter of Lloyd George's 1919 coalition, and in the 1920s Foreign Secretary. 'Twitts Ghyll' was his place to relax; in this small home Chamberlain could develop his fondness for rock plants. In his rockery were specimens from all over Europe, India, China and America. He rarely moved out of the house once he was ensconced, and only once was he known to have walked the half mile to Five Ashes hamlet and back.

A little later, in 1929, at Woodreed Farm, a retired clergyman, Rev. A. Jarvis, became one of the Sussex pioneers of silver fox breeding (others were at Balcombe, Rudgwick and Midhurst). The outlet was, of course, the fashion trade, and a writer at the time commented, 'silver fox fur bears the same relation to other furs that the diamond bears to other precious stones.' Each pair of foxes bred on average three pups, one of which was killed for its fur while the others were sold for breeding. [13]

FLETCHING

Edward Gibbon was rather passed over when we wrote *Hidden Sussex*. But his great history of *The Decline and Fall of the Roman Empire* set a new standard in accuracy and research, and has influenced almost every later writer, so he deserves a paragraph. He was born at Putney in 1737 and was educated at Westminster and Oxford. He became an MP in 1774 and two years later published the first volume of the history. After volumes 2 and 3 (1781) he went to live in Lausanne for some years, where he finished the whole vast work. On his return to England he received the friendship of the Earl of Sheffield, John Baker Holroyd (see *Sheffield Park*). Gibbon died in London, but his body was brought to Sussex and interred in the Sheffield mausoleum in Fletching church in 1794. His friend loyally compiled Gibbon's memoirs from his own notes; they were published two years later and are still of value to researchers.

Lord Sheffield's younger brother was killed on July 30, 1762, in the desperate assault on the Moro Castle in Havana, Cuba. [12]

FLIMWELL

The church was designed in 1839 by Decimus Burton, one of the most celebrated architects of his day. Though not a Sussex man, he did a great deal of work in the county, so it would be rather different today if he hadn't been around. Among other buildings, he designed St. Mary's at Goring-by-Sea, Holy Trinity church, Eastbourne, the central part of St. Leonard's (an estate for which the land was bought by his father), and the monumental eastern part of Adelaide Crescent (Hove). But Flimwell was his only village church. [7]

FOLKINGTON

The famous herbalist Nicholas Culpeper ended his days in Folkington. Born in London in 1616, he was apprenticed to an apothecary in his late teens and around 1642 set up in business as 'a student in physic and astrology'. He wrote many treatises on the art of medicine as it was then understood, but his name has become almost a by-word in the language for his *Herball*, which went through many editions.

Brock the Badger has reason to thank Lady Monckton at Folkington. In 1967 two lads who had discovered setts in the area came across an unexploded shell nearby. They called in at the nearest house to report their find and Lady Monckton, whose home it was, thereby began her great interest in these attractive animals. With her cousin, Lord Arran, she later introduced what became the Badger Protection Act in the House of Lords.   [28]

FORD

Decline and fall. The owners of the land here have included Earl Roger in 1066, Henry the Fifth in 1415 (see *Atherington*) and the noble family of Bohun. When the London merchant William Garway bought it in the late 16th century there were extensive buildings near the church and a spacious park. No longer. During the war the open acres became a leading airfield for the Battle of Britain, and now the name Ford is evocative of nothing more uplifting than one of Her Majesty's open prisons.   [18]

FOREST ROW

In 1825 the writer Horace Smith came across a ruined house in the middle of Ashdown Forest. He discovered that it had been sacked by Cromwell's troops and never rebuilt: while its owner, Sir Henry Compton, was out hunting he had heard that the Parliamentary army was approaching, so he immediately turned his horse towards the coast and the continent and never saw his home again. The story inspired Smith's novel *Brambletye House*. We've been hunting in bookshops for it for years, but probably almost all copies were thrown away as rubbish long ago.   [5]

FRAMFIELD

At the time of the English Civil War many families were divided in their loyalties. Anthony Stapley, of Framfield and Patcham, was one of the Parliamentarians who signed Charles the First's death warrant, yet his eldest son John was later part of a plot to restore Charles the Second to the throne. When discovered, he betrayed a fellow plotter, Sir Henry Slingsby, who consequently lost his head on Tower Hill, but John himself was pardoned by Cromwell for his father's sake.

Richard Realf was born here on June 14, 1834, and began writing verses at the age of 15. A volume of these was published in 1852, by which time he was studying agriculture. He soon emigrated to America, where he worked as a missionary in the slums of New York before going west to Kansas. Here he started a newspaper and met John Brown, in whose ill-fated 'provisional government' he was named as Secretary of State. When the American War of Secession broke out, Realf joined the 88th Illinois Regiment of the Federal Army and wrote a number of war songs which gained great popularity, being sung around army camp fires. He became commandant of a coloured regiment and in 1864 left the army as a lieutenant-colonel. After this he resumed his old life as journalist until, on October 28, 1878, he committed suicide as a result of domestic difficulties culminating in divorce.   **[13]**

FRANT

Two connections with uprisings here. Three of Jack Cade's followers (see *Cade Street*) came from Frant: Robert Langley, William Appes and William Bodyll. All were pardoned. Centuries later — in November, 1830, with the 'Swing riots' breaking out in south eastern England — a Frant baker, James Poulter, attempted to stir up the people in a demand for higher wages for farm workers. A mob marched on Eridge Castle, intending to besiege it, but they were poorly organised and the leaders were arrested. In East Sussex as a whole nine men were sentenced to death, 457 were transported and 400 imprisoned. Poulter got off with a two months prison sentence.

Behind the church, in a position where it's not easily seen, stands a monument to Captain Hans Busk, who was born in 1816. He was the originator of the old Volunteer Army, which eventually became the Territorial Army.

Another long-term resident of Frant was Viscount Stratford de Redcliffe, who was first cousin to George Canning, Prime Minister in the time of George the Fourth, and himself British Ambassador to Washington and in Turkey. He built Frant Court in 1859 and lived there until his death at the age of 92 in 1880.

In the early years of this century Frant was the home of the sculptor Frank Rosier, who carved (mostly in wood) beautiful screens for several Sussex churches, besides choir stalls, a reredos and a war memorial for Frant.   **[6]**

FRISTON

The music of Frank Bridge is enjoying a revival of interest. Bridge was born at Brighton in 1879 and died at Eastbourne in 1941. He is buried at Friston, and there is a memorial to him in the church. He started as conductor of the New Symphony Orchestra and later was a regular deputy for Sir Henry Wood at the 'Proms', on the rare occasions when Sir Henry was indisposed. Bridge wrote many works for chamber ensembles, and his suite, 'The Sea' remains a popular orchestral piece. He was a fine teacher, noting Benjamin Britten as a pupil.

Vicar here from 1908 to 1929 was Rev. A.A. Evans, author of *On Foot in Sussex, By Weald and Down,* and other equally charming books.   [28]

FULKING

The storage house of Fulking waterworks, with its tiled quotation from the Bible, was noted in *Hidden Sussex*. Further east is another fountain, with a red marble tablet. It's in honour of John Ruskin, Victorian writer and artist. Ruskin's interests included geology, and he had friends in Fulking who begged him to use his knowledge and his influence to get them a proper water supply. Ruskin came to the rescue, and grateful villagers subscribed to the placing here of a memento to him.   [20]

FUNTINGTON

William Scardevyle (does his name mean scare-devil?) of Funtington in 1408 headed a group of villagers who petitioned the bishop of Exeter for leave to bury their dead at Funtington instead of Bosham, on the ground that their chapel was over two miles from Bosham, and that in winter the latter place was hard to reach over the crude roads of those days. Perhaps the bishop himself had had experience of Sussex roads, but anyway the petition was granted.

In Funtington House lived for some years Admiral Sir Provo Wallis, who died in 1892 aged nearly 101. Back in 1813 he had been serving on the 'Shannon' at the time of her duel with the 'Chesapeake' on June 1. The 'Chesapeake' was a frigate of the U.S. Navy during the war of 1812. You can read the story in Winston Churchill's *History of the English Speaking Peoples,* vol. 3.   [30]

GLYNDE

Colonel Herbert Morley, grandson of the man who built Glynde Place in 1569, was a Roundhead during the Civil War and was a judge at the trial of Charles the First. He refused to sign the death warrant, a fact which was later remembered: he was allowed to buy a pardon for his Parliamentary activities.

William Hay, born at Glyndebourne in 1695, was a remarkable man. Though seriously deformed, well under five feet in height, with a hump back and misshapen limbs, he notched up a whole string of achievements including being elected as a Member of Parliament for Seaford. He travelled widely, was chairman of the Quarter Sessions and Keeper of the Records at the Tower of London. He married happily, brought up a family of five children and still found time to write essays and poetry and to translate several old Latin authors.

A later William Hay of Glyndebourne was one of three Englishmen who met a brutal death at Patna, India, during the troubles of 1763, being 'by the order of Cossam Ally Kawn and under the direction of one Someroo, an apostate European, deliberately and inhumanly murdered'. The incident is recorded on a memorial in St. Mary's church, Eastbourne.

John Ellman, who developed the Southdown breed of sheep, exported rams to Russia. Ellman was a founder of the famous Smithfield Show as well as of the Sussex County Agricultural Society. When he retired from farming in 1829 he was presented by 186 noblemen and farmers from all over the county with a massive silver tureen surmounted by the model of a Southdown sheep.

Tom Eager of Glynde was much taken with the Biblical story of Methuselah and came to the conclusion that his longevity derived from the absence of cooks in ancient times. Mr Eager therefore dispensed with the services of his housekeeper and lived on a primitive diet of bread and cheese. He died in 1845 at the age of 72 — just 897 years short of Methuselah's span!

The opera house at Glyndebourne is now so well established as a rural venue for uppercrust music lovers that it's easy to forget how doubtful the enterprise seemed when John Christie opened it in 1934. He created it as a stage for his wife, the operatic soprano Audrey Mildmay.   [21]

GOLDEN CROSS

The former postmill here (its roundhouse now attractively incorporated in a modern house) was one of many built, modified or repaired by the Medhurst brothers, Samuel and William, during the 19th century. They've been credited with developing the Sussex tailpole fan tackle, an example of which was installed at Golden Cross. This harnesses the wind to move the mill around its post into the optimum position for the sails to do their work. Previously the miller had to move the tailpole by hand. [22]

GOODWOOD

In 1768 the naturalist Gilbert White (see also *Nyewood*) came to Goodwood to see a moose which the Duke of Richmond had imported and was keeping in the park. Alas! the animal died the day before White arrived. All the same, one of the letters in *The Natural History of Selborne* is almost entirely devoted to it: 'though it had been dead for so short a time, it was in so putrid a state that the stench was hardly supportable'. [17]

GORING

Richard Jefferies (1848-87), author of many books in which a keen observation of the natural world is processed through a poetic and philosophical sensibility, lived in Sussex for some years and came to Goring for his last months. He lived in a house called Sea View, now re-named Jefferies House, in a lane south of the church. He's buried in Broadwater Cemetery. In a couple of sentences Jefferies summarises the best of this world:
"The exceeding beauty of the earth, in her splendour of life,
yields a new thought with every petal. The hours when the mind
is absorbed by beauty are the only hours when we really live." [19]

GRAFFHAM

During the early 19th century a footman named Allen in the service of the Lennox family turned footpad and infested the roads around Arundel and Chichester. He relieved farmers of their purses as they returned from market, and his daring made him the terror of western Sussex. Eventually the militia were called out to try to capture him, and they got so close on his trail that he was forced to take refuge in a pond at Graffham. Here he was spotted by a group of his pursuers including one Captain Sargent. Allen was called upon to give himself up, but his only reply was a shot which killed Sargent on the instant. The soldiers thereupon opened fire and killed Allen in his turn. The story does, however, have a happier side: Sargent had two heiresses, as to whose story see *Woolavington*. [9]

GRAVETYE

The first owners of Gravetye Manor were named Inningfield or Infield. Richard Infield is known to have died there in 1571. The manor gradually sank in the world until 1884, when it was bought by William Robinson. He was, however, more interested in the grounds — all one thousand acres of them. Robinson was a pioneer of the English natural garden, and he planted many hundreds of trees and shrubs, creating a variety of landscapes. In 1911 he wrote a classic book, *Gravetye Manor, or Twenty Years' Work round an Old Manor-house*, in which he told of the ways in which he fought Nature to produce a masterpiece. He died at Gravetye, well into his nineties, in 1935. The Gardens were neglected in the ensuing War, but the William Robinson Trust has preserved much of the landscape and the view from the house. [5]

GREATHAM

Alice and Wilfred Meynell, husband and wife both authors, lived here, well away from the hustle of town life. Alice's first poems were published in 1875, her last almost fifty years later, and she is still read with affection. Her best-remembered lyric is probably the one which begins:

> She walks — the lady of my delight —
> A shepherdess of sheep.
> Her flocks are thoughts. She keeps them white;
> She guards them from the steep.

In 1915 Viola Meynell lent D. H. Lawrence a cottage here, where he completed his novel *The Rainbow* and had E. M. Forster and Bertrand Russell among his visitors. [9/10]

GROOMBRIDGE

Taking hostages and holding them for huge ransoms is not an invention of the 20th century. Five hundred years ago Groombridge manor belonged to Richard Waller, who had spent much time in France, fighting French and Burgundians. He was fortunate enough to take as hostage Jean, Count of Angoulême and uncle of the future Louis XII, whom he brought back to Groombridge and kept there from 1412 to 1445 — a third of a century — before Jean was released when his ransom was paid. [6]

GUESTLING

About a mile outside the village lies Maxfield, the house where, about 1540, was born Gregory Martin, author and Catholic scholar. He became tutor to the children of Thomas Howard, the then Duke of Norfolk. Later he crossed the Channel to Douai and the Catholic church. In the 1570s he, with two helpers, translated the Bible from the Vulgate into English, a version known as the Douai or Rheims Bible. Dying on October 28, 1582, he was buried at Rheims.

The Cheyney family lived at Guestling, and tradition tells that they and the Oxenbridges at *Brede* were perpetually feuding. Once it's said that a party of Cheyneys surprised an Oxenbridge in bed and slew him on the spot! [24]

HADLOW DOWN

It is on record that a farmer named Bridger wanted to have his son christened Beelzebub. The parson refused to carry out such a request, so the boy was named Augustus. Seeing how children can take the mickey out of their afflicted contemporaries, no doubt Augustus was duly grateful. **[13]**

HAILSHAM

We of the 'enlightened' twentieth century cannot but feel sorry for the unfortunate women who in sixteenth century and earlier times were condemned as witches. But a record of East Grinstead Assizes poses a different problem; was Joan Usbarne Mrs. or Miss?

> "1572. At the Assizes at East Grinstead, Joan Usbarne at Hailsham, spinster, wife of John Usbarne of Hailsham, bewitched to death one bull value 40s. of the goods and chattels of John Browne. Sentence one year."

A brewer of a later age in Hailsham was sufficient of an expert at his work to inspire a poem by John Hollamby, from which we give the last two verses:

> *"The meagre French their thirst would quench,*
> *And find much good 'twould do them;*
> *Keep them a year on Gooche's beer,*
> *Their country would not know them.*
>
> *All you that have not tasted it*
> *I'd have you set about it; —*
> *No man with pence and commonsense*
> *Would ever be without it."*   **[22]**

HALLAND

The Pelham family (see *Introduction*) acquired the estate in Tudor times, and during the reign of Elizabeth I a vast mansion was built as the principal family seat. It was the scene of lavish hospitality, especially during the time of Thomas Pelham-Holles, first Duke of Newcastle. After his death in 1768 the building was dismantled and used as a source of building materials.

The Duke joined Walpole's ministry in 1724 and served with loyalty, even though not with great distinction. In 1739 as a member of the Cabinet he was leader of a group who advocated war against Spain, contrary to Walpole's own wishes. The rebels got their way and eventually Walpole was defeated, handing in his resignation in February 1742. In the following year Henry Pelham, the Duke's brother, was made principal minister, although the Duke himself wielded the greater power in spite of the uncomfortable fact that he was of a petty disposition and timid character. In 1754 the Duke became principal minister and in 1756 declared war on France — an action which forced him to an humilating resignation before the Peace of Paris in 1763. Still, he left over 300 volumes of correspondence, mostly concerned with the maintenance of patronage, on which he depended for political survival. **[22]**

HALNAKER

Before a General Post Office was created, mail was carried by local or long-distance coaches and riders. Deliveries from main towns, which had a postmaster, were made to a 'receiver' appointed from each smaller community. At Halnaker a 'receiving house' was approved in 1808, a Mr. White being made Receiver. By 1822 the Receiver was Mr. Moore, who was sacked the next year because he was regularly unable to balance his books. At the time the Chichester postmaster was a Mr. Angel, and he without consent appointed his own daughter as Halnaker Receiver. The postal charge from Chichester to Halnaker was one penny, but Miss Angel charged an extra penny without any authority. Local feeling was so strong that lengthy petitions were got up against Miss Angel, who seems to have thoroughly belied her name!

Sir William Morley, Chichester MP in the mid-seventeenth century, had a daughter Mary, who inherited Halnaker House and married the Earl of Derby in 1704. She founded an almshouse for twelve poor widows (whom she described as 'aged maidens'), one of whom was required to instruct local girls in the arts of reading and needlework. She died in 1752, aged 84. After her death Halnaker House, one of the most intriguingly secluded Sussex homes, ceased to be used as a residence. It fell into decay and much of its stone was used for farm buildings and metalling roads. There's a house in Chichester which, it's claimed, was entirely faced with Halnaker stone.   [17]

HAMMERPOT

The fowl decoy belonging to the Dukes of Norfolk was remembered in *Hidden Sussex*. Its beginning is lost in the mists of time — in the early 19th century it was said to have existed 'from time immemorial'. It was only small, but was capable of large catches. Once in the early 19th century it achieved a total of 90 head of wildfowl in a single day, which must have kept the Arundel castle kitchens busy. The decoyman then was George Knight — he held this post for sixty years, dying, still active, at the age of 91.   [19]

HAMMERWOOD

Benjamin Henry Latrobe was not born here, but he gave the village its finest house. Born in 1764, he was a student of the architect Cockerell. Hammerwood House (dated 1793) was his first independent commission. Two years later he emigrated to Norfolk, Virginia, U.S.A., and in the course of time became perhaps the most eminent architect of his day in the new world. As Surveyor of Public Buildings from 1803 he was in charge of the completion of the two Chambers of the Capitol in Washington. He profoundly improved the whole architectural profession in America, and is now proudly claimed as an American architect. But he began his career here in Sussex.   [5]

HAMSEY

The history of Coombe House goes back to at least 1497 — probably much earlier — but for over 300 years it has been the home of the Bridger family. Col. Richard Bridger JP. bought it in 1657. He became M.P. for Lewes in 1679, holding the seat for fifteen years. His great-grandson John was knighted at the time of the coronation of King George III. John's daughter married George Shiffner, who was created a baronet and also represented Lewes in Parliament for many years. In the twentieth century, Sir Henry Shiffner, still a local man, was killed in action in the western desert in 1941. And even in 1985 a Shiffner is still connected to the Lewes telephone exchange. [21]

HANDCROSS

Sussex has some wonderful gardens, and some gardening families worthy of thanks for opening their creations to the general public. It was Ludwig Messel who began to develop the thirty acres of Nymans in 1889, importing such exotic plants as rhododendrons, azaleas and hydrangeas. He planted a pinetum, created a sunken garden, a heather garden, a walled garden and much else. His son Leonard greatly enlarged the cultivated area and the collection between the wars, and although the property is now owned by the National Trust it has long been managed by Leonard's daughter, the Countess of Rosse. [4]

HANGLETON

On November 1, 1792, a fourteen-year-old boy, Ryall John Stevenson, who was the Steyning postboy, was stopped by two men named Rook and Howell — the latter was a tailor by trade. They grabbed the mailbags and ran off. However, they had been seen acting suspiciously and were arrested. They were brought before the 1793 Lent Assizes, convicted of mail robbery and executed. Their bodies were then, in accordance with the fashion of the time, hung upon gibbets at the scene of the crime until they rotted. The story goes that Rook's mother visited the gibbet each night and collected her son's bones as they fell to the ground one by one. Then she buried them secretly in consecrated ground at Old Shoreham. Lord Tennyson was so struck by this tale of maternal devotion that he wrote a ballad about it, called 'Rizpah'. It isn't often found in anthologies, but of course it figures in the poet's complete works. Here is a snatch of it:

> *Do you think I was scared by the bones? I kissed 'em, I buried 'em all —*
> *I can't dig deep, I am old — in the night by the churchyard wall.*
> *My Willy'll rise up whole when the trumpet of judgment'll sound,*
> *But I charge you never to say that I laid him in holy ground.* [20]

HANKHAM

Back in the 1950s the owner of Peelings Manor, Kenneth Banner, made a startling discovery: beneath the false walls, paint and plaster of centuries there lay hidden a medieval open hall. He might never have realised just what he had unearthed but for an unknown visitor who declared himself interested in old buildings and who proceeded, albeit with great modesty, to point out all the tell-tale features of the place. We enjoy this story because it yields us a glimpse at his researches of a man whose work lies behind books like our own. When he departed Peelings he left his calling card: he was Nikolaus Pevsner.

[23]

HARDHAM

One of the strangest legal actions ever started had its origins here. In 1272 the Prior of Hardham, whose name was Richard, had a lawsuit brought against him by Milane, the anchoress at Steyning, claiming that he owed her 5,600 loaves of bread, 5,600 cooked messes and 6,800 gallons of ale. One can't help wondering what she would have done with it all, had the Prior fulfilled a judgement against him for these quantities.

The priors of Hardham were, many of them, unconventional to say the least. Prior Richard in 1285 himself became an anchorite — the cell may have been the first reason why a squint was built in the church. Prior Robert was in 1299 deposed for misrule, incontinence and adultery. In 1355 John de Kent was sent off to Tortington so that he could have time to 'refrain from worldly matters and attend to spiritual'. In 1478 Prior Henry kept bad order and the brethren were given to frequenting neighbouring taverns. And in 1524 Prior Robert was compelled to admit that he'd been one of a party of men who stole the Earl of Arundel's deer.

[9]

HARTFIELD

Every Good Friday morning at ten o'clock there's a short service by the grave of Nicholas 'Beggarman' Smith in Hartfield churchyard. This is a remarkable survival from the early 17th century. Smith, a wealthy man, apparently travelled far through Sussex looking for somewhere to put down roots, but in every place he visited he was given a cold welcome. Until, that is, he came to Hartfield, where he was warmly received. He settled at Crotchford Manor and in his will of October 18, 1634 he gave £10 to be shared in perpetuity between forty poor people of the parish. Oddly, in Horsfield's *History of Sussex,* the learned author says it was £5 and the distribution was to be on Christmas Day; but we prefer to stick to the parish history written by Rev. P.D.S. Blake.

Nicholas must not be confused with his near-contemporary Henry 'Dog' Smith, whom we note under *Warbleton*. Henry died on January 3, 1627 and is buried at Wandsworth.

[29]

HARTING

Several colourful characters have been associated with the great house called Uppark. Lord Grey, who had it built around 1690, was one of the leaders of the Monmouth rebellion, was captured and was lucky to escape with a hefty fine. He was also involved in a scandal of another sort, running off with his wife's eighteen-year-old sister, Lady Henrietta Berkely, and being hauled before the courts for the offence.

Sir Harry Fetherstonhaugh, who owned the house in Regency times, was known for extravagances of various kinds. His parties were prodigious and it's

said that, after feasting in the so-called Vandalian Tower (you can see its remains from the car park), guests would be trundled back to the house in wheelbarrows. The Prince Regent, with whom he later fell out, was a frequent visitor, and his bed can still be seen here. In 1780 Sir Harry brought a beautiful but uneducated country girl to Uppark — the eighteen-year-old Emma Hart. She evidently threw herself into the spirit of his festivities, since there's a record of her dancing on the dining table. Unhappily, when she became pregnant Sir Harry sent her away virtually penniless. The end of the story? By no means: Emma was to find wealthy friends, and she became Nelson's Lady Hamilton.

Although Sir Harry later retired from public life to improve his house and grounds (Humphrey Repton being his chief adviser) his eye for a pretty face hadn't clouded. He was past 70 when he fell in love with his head dairy maid, Mary Ann Bullock. He sent her to Paris to be educated after their marriage and they lived happily together for a further 21 years.

H.G. Wells lived here for a time, as his mother became housekeeper in 1850. The underground passages at the house (an unusual 'below stairs' device for the servants to do their work out of sight) gave him the idea of the subterranean civilization for his book *The Time Machine*.

Before the present house was built there was an earlier one here, the home of the Ford family. Sir Edward Ford, in the mid-17th century, was a 'philosopher', in the days when anyone was so called who had an enquiring turn of mind. He has his place in history as the first person to succeed in raising water by pumping.

Another man who earns an historical niche is John Rickman, clerk of the House of Commons, who in 1803 married Susanna Postlethwaite of Harting. He drew up the plan for the very first national census. **[29]**

82

HASSOCKS

A good old Sussex family were the Saxbys, who came from Maresfield, and of whom some went to America with the Pilgrim Fathers. But John Saxby, who lived at Hassocks in the mid-nineteenth century, was interested in a different form of transport — railways. He worked for nearly a quarter of a century for the London Brighton & South Coast Railway and produced a steady stream of ingenious inventions. In the days when signalling and point-changing was all done by hand, one of the commonest causes of accidents was for the man in the signal-box to change the points just as a train was going over them. But Saxby put paid to that by inventing a system of interlocking signals and points, so that you couldn't pull the points lever unless the signals were in a safe position. Later he started up his own business at Haywards Heath, still making signal-box equipment. He prospered so much that he was forced to move to Kilburn, and by the time he closed down he was running similar businesses in Belgium and France.   [20]

HEATHFIELD

We mentioned General Elliott, created Lord Heathfield, in *Hidden Sussex*. His descendant Mr. H. Newberry, lived at Heathfield Park and was the builder of the Gibraltar Tower — it cost him over £5,000. Newberry, who was High Sheriff of Sussex in the 1790s, was largely responsible for the quelling of serious rioting at Newhaven. The king offered him a knighthood, which he declined, and instead the king gave him a personal testimonal.

One of the most attractive Sussex artists was Jonathan Harmer, born in 1762, elder of the two sons of Jonathan Harmer, senior, stonemason of Heathfield. Jonathan junior spent three years in New York with his younger brother John. Then in 1799 he returned to Heathfield upon the death of his father and took over the family business. He specialised in the making of terra-cotta bas-reliefs to ornament the family firm's tombstones. They vary in colour from cream to a strong red, and were cast in a comparatively small number of designs — cherubs, baskets of fruit, vases, figures of Faith, Hope and Charity, and so on. His work can be found in some sixteen East Sussex churchyards, and some casts and moulds are at Anne of Cleves House Museum, Lewes. Harmer died in 1849, aged 86, and was buried in Heathfield churchyard.   [13]

HELLINGLY

Quite what young Agnes Devenish of Horselunges Manor was doing to have a plum stone lodged in her nostril we have no idea, but her prolonged discomfort led to a Sussex miracle. This was in the reign of Henry VI. It was actually feared that Agnes would die and, in desperation, her mother invoked the 'blessed king' — whereupon the stone obligingly fell out.

The Devenish family lived at Horselunges from the 1430s to the 1560s. As lords of the manor the family had certain long-ingrained rights, but the methods they used would by modern standards be open to suspicion. In 1553 one Richard Barnard of Hellingly 'feloniously as a felon did drown and destroy himself', a reminder that until quite recently suicide was illegal. Upon this sad event, Thomas Devenish appears to have seized Barnard's goods and chattels to the value of £14 as being forfeited to the lord of the manor. But after the accession of Elizabeth I the goods were claimed on behalf of the Crown by the Queen's Almoner. He brought a complaint before the Court of Star Chamber, stating one 'Thomas Devenyshe, the elder, of Hellingly, esq., and William Devenysshe, gentleman, and other riotous persons came to the mansion and dwellingplace of the said Richard, and broke and entered the same and took and carried away the said goods and chattels'.

Lord Dacre of the South (Thomas Fiennes) was a scapegrace of the time of Henry VIII. He and a group of 'gentlemen' planned to go hunting in Laughton Park, which belonged to the Pelhams, one April night. On the way from Herstmonceux to Laughton they reached Hellingly and a brawl blew up with three local men, one of whom received injuries from which he died the next day. Lord Dacre and his cronies were arraigned for murder: Dacre was brought before the Lord Chancellor and other Lords, who found him guilty. He was executed at Tyburn two days later. [22]

HENFIELD

Canon Nathaniel Woodard (d. 1891) who lived at Martyn Lodge founded Lancing, Ardingly and Hurstpierpoint colleges for educating the sons of the Sussex middle classes. The package on offer included reasonable fees, a marked Anglican atmosphere and a degree of spartan living. The schools were instrumental in the spread of association football in the county (including the founding of Brighton and Hove Albion) but they reverted to rugby because of a distaste for soccer's professionalism.

The Misses Allen-Brown ran a violet nursery here in the early years of the century. They had more than 7,000 plants under glass and everything used in the packing was coloured violet — even the string and shavings. In 1907 Queen Alexandra accepted a gift of violets in a Sussex wooden trug. The sisters also sold violet toilet soap, perfume and face cream, and grew carnations and lavender in other parts of their 4½ acres. [20]

HERSTMONCEUX

The family of de Fienes dates back to the Normans. Sir John de Fienes came over with the Conqueror and may have been his kinsman. Later Fienes became crusaders. In the 14th century Sir John de Fienes married Maud de Monceux, heiress of Herstmonceux, and they made Herst manor house their chief residence. Their great-grandson Sir Roger became Treasurer to the Household of Henry VI and the original builder of Herstmonceux Castle. He was born in the manor house and baptized in the parish church on September 14, 1384. Later he was one of the 'happy few' who fought at Agincourt. He began work on the castle in 1440, the cost of the building coming to £3,800.

At the outbreak of the first world war Lt. Col. Claude Lowther of Herstmonceux Castle raised three battalions of men which became the Southdown Battalions (the 11th, 12th and 13th) of the Royal Sussex Regiment. They were popularly known as Lowther's Lambs and had a Southdown sheep as a mascot. A.W Busbridge wrote a marching song for them, the refrain of which went:

> *For the Sussex stock is staunch,*
> *And the Sussex blood is true,*
> *And the Sussex lads are keen*
> *When there's soldier's work to do.*
> *Hear us tramp, tramp, tramp*
> *Till the country is a camp,*
> *And we start the little business*
> *We have sworn to carry through.*

The name of the village is pronounced 'Herstmon-ZOO', a fact which must have pleased the rector from 1923-56, Rosslyn Bruce. He was an animal fanatic. At Oxford he was forbidden to keep a dog in college, so he rented a cow and paraded it around the quad. Thereafter he kept all kinds of creatures, from pigeons to elephants, and when he travelled (by car) to his new living at Herstmonceux a goat gave birth to two kids on the way. While in Sussex he wrote books on animals, including the celebrated (in those circles) *Fox Terrier Breeding, the Line and Family Method.* His most bizarre achievement was to breed a green mouse. [23]

HEYSHOTT

We noted in *Hidden Sussex* the local associations with Richard Cobden, far too important a figure to be passed over. He was born here, but set up in business as a calico printer in Burnley. After writing some pamphlets advocating free trade he became one of the most energetic campaigners against the harsh Corn Laws, which were repealed in 1846 largely through his efforts. [8]

HICKSTEAD

Charles Fleet, writing a hundred years ago, recorded several members of the Stapley family of Hickstead Place, who kept detailed diaries of their activities between 1607 and 1743. During the 1640s and 1650s the family records contain numerous entries such as 'To the King, £1.4s.2d.' and 'To the Parliament, £1.7s.6d.' As Fleet commented, 'the contribution to King and Parliament is pretty equal, and perhaps the feelings of the Stapleys were pretty equally balanced. All that they cared for was to be let alone!' [11]

HIGHBROOK

A tale of local benefactors. In 1875 Mr and Mrs Kirby of Highbrook House built a schoolroom (now the parish hall) which was also used for religious services until, in 1884, Mr Stephenson Clarke of Hook Farm gave the parish land and building stone for a church. Mrs Kirby gave £2,500 in railway debentures to form a fund for the incumbent's stipend and, in 1887, Mr Clarke gave the present peal of bells and a splendid carillon to commemorate Queen Victoria's Golden Jubilee. The carillon plays a range of tunes which drift cheerfully across the Weald. On the day we were last there it was offering 'Home, Sweet Home', perfectly played despite the instrument's great age.   [12]

HIGHDOWN

Isolated on the windswept downland about a quarter of a mile north of the A2032 Worthing to Littlehampton road is the tomb of John Olliver, who once owned a postmill here. He began to prepare for his death in 1766 when he was 57, keeping his coffin safely stowed under his bed; though

he perhaps surprised himself by surviving to the age of 84. The funeral was to his own specifications. The mourners (all two thousand of them) were dressed in colourful clothing, and the burial service was read by a young girl.
[19]

HIGH SALVINGTON

The great lawyer John Selden, born here in 1584, amassed a substantial fortune of £40,000 which he bequeathed to his four executors, apart from legacies of a mere £100 each to his sister's children. Selden told friends that he had 'nobody to make his heir but a milkmayd, and that such people did not know what to do with a great estate'. [19]

HOLLINGTON

After the old church of St Leonards was washed away by the sea the parish of Hollington laid claim to jurisdiction over at least part of the neighbouring territory. In the 17th century the parsons of Hollington used to baptize St Leonards children and prepare them for confirmation — and not always with good grace. Richard Russell, for example, wrote in the church register in 1671: 'Married, John Harmore and Widow Ashby, both of the *reputed* parish of St Leonards'. Four years later he wrote, even more belligerently, 'John Tharp of the *pretended* parish of St Leonards'. [24]

HOLTYE

We referred in *Hidden Sussex* to the short length of Roman road here. It was excavated and researched in 1939 by one of the county's great archaeologists, Ivan D. Margary. He was a member of the Council of Sussex Archaeological Society for some 40 years and was its chairman for 18 of them. He was particularly known for his research on Roman roads in Britain, most during the years after the second world war, and his book *Roman Roads in Britain* is unlikely ever to be superseded. His report on the Holtye road appears in volume 81 of the Sussex Archaeological Collections. [5]

HOOE

An 18th century landlord of the Red Lion, James Blackman, was a member of the Groombridge gang of smugglers and took convoys of contraband to Ashdown Forest. In 1744 three Jacobites came to him for help when they were trying to reach France and join the Pretender, Bonnie Prince Charlie, but it seems that Blackman betrayed them and they were arrested here.

Nathaniel Torriano, an incumbent of the church in the mid-18th century, had been a physician before taking holy orders and was interested in the more violent natural phenomena. He earned considerable fame when in 1756 he preached a sermon after the great Lisbon earthquake. It was subsequently printed and widely circulated at the time, though copies are very rare nowadays. [23]

HORAM

Formerly Horeham, the big house was built by Thomas Dyke in the time of James I. He, his wife Joan and their eldest son Abraham, all died in the space of ten months in 1632. A descendant, Sir John Dyke, demolished most of the house in the 18th century and used the materials to build a cottage at Southbourne. [22]

HORSEBRIDGE

James McDougall had a mill here around the turn of the century. He was the grandson of Alexander McDougall, a simple miller who founded a great business. James himself went on to become chairman of the company which makes the flour many of us buy for our home baking.[22]

HORSTED KEYNES

One of the most fascinating documents about Sussex that we still have from the remoter past is the diary kept by Giles Moore, rector here from 1655 until his death in 1679. Arthur J. Rees well describes him: 'A choleric, sometimes almost a bombastic figure, he comes to life in the pages of his diary as a bluff and hearty clergyman, quick to anger but kind of heart. He denounces an erring maid-servant of his household as a 'whoare', but marries her to her sweetheart and gives her gifts worth her year's wages at the wedding feast'. Thomas Hinde notes in his engaging *Field Guide to the English Country Parson* that Moore's jottings chiefly consist of a record of the cost of living. When his brother sickened Moore showed an interest in the details of his will. Eventually, in a high fever, this brother 'leaped into a well which was ten feete deep in water, out of which he was quickly taken and put into a warme bed'. He died soon afterwards and, as Hinde quietly observes, 'Moore costs his funeral'. [12]

HOUGHTON

We've mentioned Charles II's escape under *Bramber*, but he and Colonel Gounter had earlier visited the George and Dragon at Houghton, where they ate 'neat's tongues' and drank a stoop of ale. The pub is still here.

James Goble was the local madcap of the early 19th century. He's recorded as having run along the top of hawthorn hedges against youths on terra firma, and as having often beaten them. He was given the nickname 'Lord Moon', perhaps because of his propensity to grab the vanes of windmills and go round with the sweeps. Once he did this at Amberley mill in a high wind and was thrown clear over a sixteen foot fence. [18]

HUNSTON

Nowadays gifts of specific items in wills are usually confined to valuables such as furniture and jewellery. It wasn't always so. In 1538 Thomas Gobel of Hunston left 'to Our Lady brotherhood of the same church, one bushel of wheat'. Our guess is that it was distributed to the poor.   [25]

HURST GREEN

At 13, Richard Russell may be the youngest highwayman on record, though the precise details of his felony haven't come down to us. What we do know is that he robbed the Hurst Green Mail 'of a draft value £32 14s, the property of James Bourn of Mountfield'. He was charged at the assizes in 1796 and was, 'in consideration of his tender age, indicted only for a misdemeanor of which he was found guilty and ordered to be imprisoned for a term of six months'.

Many smugglers were by no means creatures of romance but hard-bitten and ruthless men. George Chapman was a member of the vicious Hawkhurst Gang, and he was gibbeted in his home village of Hurst Green for the murder of Thomas Carswell in 1744.   [15]

HURSTPIERPOINT

The 'One Thumb white boss', alias missionary Bishop James Hannington from Hurstpierpoint, was killed by the natives in Eastern Equatorial Africa at the age of 38. The son of the man who founded the Brighton store, he'd been curate in charge at St George's Church in Hurstpierpoint and a strong preacher against the demon drink, before joining the Church Missionary Society. As the first Bishop of Eastern Equatorial Africa he led several expeditions there, until in 1885 the German annexation of their territory led the natives to distrust the intentions of all white men. Only four of Hannington's 50-strong party escaped the resulting massacre. And the 'One Thumb' soubriquet? When he was nine years old he tried to dispose of a wasps' nest at St George's — with a home-made bomb. His left thumb was blown off.

Almost incredibly, the village has in its time produced no fewer than four famous bishops — Awdry, Greaves and Montgomery as well as Hannington.

The present church is Victorian, and the designs were by Sir Charles Barry who created the Houses of Parliament. It was the gift of the Borrer family who lived at Pakyns Manor. The first record is that Pakyns was inherited by William Borrer, who was High Sherriff of Sussex in 1802. His eldest son, William, was a famous botanist, who wrote a number of books (with his own illustrations) which are still in demand today.   [20]

ICKLESHAM

How Joan Tokye lived isn't recorded, but she surely departed this world in style. Her will instructed that 'ii busshells of malte be equivally devyded betwyxt John Tokye and John Garlye so that they twoo buy me a fyrkyng of bere at the day of my buryall'.

The Victorian painter Millais had an uncomfortable moment in Icklesham church. During his sermon the vicar decided to use his illustrious visitor as an example of Man's limitations compared with the power of his Creator. Leaning from the pulpit, he asked — rhetorically, it must have been — whether Millais could reproduce some spiritual quality. 'No, my brethren,' he continued briskly and conclusively, 'he cannot paint that!' [24]

IDEN

Families often took their surnames from the place where they lived in medieval times. The Idens lived here for two centuries and more, one of them being the John Alexander Iden who captured Jack Cade (see *Cade Street*). They're supposed to have lived at a house called The Moat, about a mile west of the village. Horsfield in 1835 reported that 'the building is now no longer in existence', but in the current Ordnance maps an old moat is still shown adjacent to Moat Farm, so history still lingers. [16]

IFIELD

Compulsory retirement isn't an exclusively modern phenomenon. Sir John de Ifelde, born around 1265, held many offices of greater importance in those times than they would be considered today — he was a Commissioner of Array, for instance, and a Commissioner of Marshes in Sussex. He was made a knight in 1324 but 13 years later was excused from active duty by the king as he was over 70. This was said to be 'against his will'.

Thomas de Yffeld's daughter Salerne was saved from suicide by a miracle. She purloined a cheese from the family larder, and was made to feel so guilty by her mother that she lowered herself into a well. As a result of a servant's calling to her she let go of the edge, calling on St Thomas. The saint appeared to her and miraculously provided two beams across the width of the well, where she could rest with feet and hands until rescued. [4]

IFOLD

John Napper was made chairman of the Guardians of the Petworth Union — a euphemistic term for the workhouse — in the year that the young Queen Victoria mounted the throne. Thirty years later he was still in office, having shown wisdom and benevolence all that time, so his colleagues raised a fund in the area to present him with a suitable testimonial. But John Napper wouldn't hear of it: he added a good slice of his own money to the fund and in 1869 it was all spent in building a new schoolhouse at nearby Plaistow. A small tablet records his generosity. [2]

IFORD

Hugo de Plaiz was the man responsible for what's thought to be the first windmill referred to anywhere in England. The year was 1155. Hugo 'gave to the monks of Lewes, the windmill in his manor of Iford, for the health of the soul of his father'.

A forgotten literary figure and a friend of the great Dr Johnson was John Delap. He was ordained about 1750, inducted into the united benefices of Iford and Kingston in 1765 and made rector of Woolavington in 1774. He used to call on the Thrales during their Sussex visits, and through them he got to know Johnson and Fanny Burney. Delap fancied himself as a tragedian and when his play *Hecuba* was produced at Drury Lane in 1761 Garrick, no less, spoke the Prologue and wrote the Epilogue. But Delap had a string of flops and unacted plays and, moreover, was something of a trial to his acquaintances because of his hypochondria. Johnson castigated him 'for dwelling too much on his internal complaints'.

[21]

IPING

Sir Charles Hamilton, lord of the manor here, was a colonel of the Scots Guards during the Crimean War. He survived the bloody battle of Alma in 1854 and lived to the age of 81. After his death in 1891 a commemorative east window was installed in the church. This includes figures of Joshua and St. John which have since changed places. Architectural etiquette decrees that Old Testament characters should appear on one side of Christ, New Testament on the other; the artist made a mistake at Iping and this was later corrected.

[8]

ISFIELD

English spelling, even of surnames, settled down only in fairly recent times and the Shurleys of Isfield were a branch of the Shirley family of Wiston. In *Hidden Sussex* we refer to the many monuments in the church. In the early 17th century Elizabeth Palmer, daughter of Sir John Shurley, achieved an obstetric feat which has probably never been equalled: she gave birth to three sons on three successive Sundays!

Stories of men beating their wives were commonplace in the 18th century, but one hears less of wives getting their own back. After a man named Baldock got drunk and beat his wife, seventeen of the village women seized him and tossed him in a blanket until they were too exhausted to go on. Encouraged by the cries of the crowd they then threw him into the horse pond.

[12/21]

ITCHINGFIELD

Few Sussex villages can boast the continued residence of a single family for as long as Itchingfield. The earliest record of the Merlotts is in 1300, when Emma Merlott was married to Thomas de Mundham, or Muntham. Then we find that in 1375 William Merlot(t) acquired Muntham Manor when he married Emma atte Hurst — the name probably means that she was born at Hurstpierpoint. At Agincourt in 1415 William Merlotte of 'Etchynfeld' was one of 27 men of arms under Sir Thomas Hoo. There's a feasible tradition that bows cut from the yews in Itchingfield churchyard were used at Agincourt. After the battle William went back to the village, and his descendants maintained the connection right down to October 1812 when Miss Elizabeth Merlott, last of the line, sold her manorial rights, and after more than 500 years the name at last died out.

In 1714 the man nicknamed 'the battle-axe of Sussex' was buried in the churchyard. He was Matthew Caffin, a Baptist preacher who was imprisoned no fewer than four times for his religion.

Sir Hector Maclean was a valiant supporter of the Old Pretender in 1715, and when the rebellion failed he sought sanctuary with his old friend Alexander Hay, who was rector here. Hay allowed him to hide in Itchingfield church, but he was discovered, hauled off and executed. As a warning to others his head was placed on a beam in the roof. During the restoration of the church in 1865 the architect Sir Gilbert Scott removed the casing from some of the old beams and found a skull resting up there. Was it old Sir Hector's?[3]

JARVIS BROOK

Not all ghosts are white! The road between the village and nearby Crowborough used to be haunted not by a spectral human or a grisly hound but by an inanimate object — to wit, a bag of soot! Jacqueline Simpson, in *The Folklore of Sussex*, reports that a local blacksmith was accosted by this bag of soot one night and chased all the way to his front door. The story is so improbable that we feel it must be true.   [6]

JEVINGTON

James Lambert, born here of humble parents in 1725, became one of the best painters of heraldic devices, and especially of pub signs. Commissioned by Sir William Burrell to depict the antiquities of Sussex, he produced a series of admirable water-colours, running into several hundreds. He was also a fine musician and for many years the regular organist at St Thomas-at-Cliffe, Lewes.

During the first world war there was a Royal Naval air station at Polegate, from which airships patrolled the English channel, and on December 22, 1917, there was a tragedy at Jevington. One of the airships, returning to base in a night fog, mistook one of its sister ships for the lights of the radio tower and came down on top of it. Two of the heroes of the night, air mechanic Harold Robinson and boy mechanic Eric Steer, ran to the burning remains of the airship and removed the bombs. This saved the lives of the injured crewmen and Robinson and Steer were both awarded the Albert Medal.   [28]

KEYMER

There used to be a large pond here and below it stood a mill — probably one of the two mentioned in Domesday. One of the occupants of the mill house had an unforgettable experience on an occasion during the 1820s when the pond's retaining wall gave way and the waters rushed right through the house. Everything was carried off by the tidal wave, including a bed upon which an unsuspecting woman was resting. Poor soul, she can hardly have expected to go for a boat trip in such an unlikely craft! But there's a happy ending, because the surge of the waters gradually abated and her bed came to rest against the branches of an overhanging tree, leaving her wet and shocked, but no worse.

An incident near Stone Pound crossroads on the night of December 1, 1802, has been interpreted in different ways, but the common elements in all the stories are that an exciseman confronted a group of smugglers, one man was shot dead, and that the villain of the piece was one Bob Bignall, or Bignell. Bignall, himself a smuggler though he had apparently turned informer on this occasion, shot a young man called Webber with a pistol. He escaped the noose this time but was hanged a few years later after terrorising the neighbourhood and threatening the life of the landlord of the White Horse at Ditchling. [20]

KINGSFOLD

Mr and Mrs Langridge from Kingsfold can lay claim to be the last of the traditional charcoal burner families in Sussex — and probably in the entire country. Mr Langridge learned the art from his father-in-law, Jim Francis, who was still making charcoal in earth kilns in 1948, and twenty years after this the Langridges re-lived old times by reconstructing a camp at the Weald and Downland Open Air Museum at Singleton. Because the kilns had to be watched day and night, the charcoal burners always lived in turf huts on the site, and Mrs Langridge knew no other kind of home until she was sixteen. 'Mrs Langridge's only complaint,' records the museum guide, 'is that it was difficult to dry clothes. Every Sunday the best clothes were brought out of a chest and the whole family went to sing with the Salvation Army, of which her father was a staunch supporter.' [3]

KINGSTON (East Sussex)

In *Hidden Sussex* we mentioned the small building with domed roof where Kingston Lane meets the A27. By tradition the ill-fated Nan Kemp was the toll-keeper here at the beginning of the 18th century. Nan was reputed to have killed her infant child and tried unsuccessfully to burn it. She then committed suicide in this little building. A kind of tumulus or mound north of the village used to be known as Nan Kemp's grave, the thought being that she was buried in unconsecrated ground because of her crimes (*see illustration on page 161*).

[21]

KINGSTON (West Sussex)

In July 1735 a party of excise officers was given a tip-off that a cargo of brandy was to be run in to shore here. On going to meet it, they were confronted by a gang of ten smugglers. One started to brandish a pistol, but the excisemen overcame the gang, seized the brandy and carried it off to the customs house. On this occasion the law prevailed, but all too often it didn't. Smugglers would either bribe or overawe the excise officers, who left them alone. So the law-abiding inhabitants of many seaside villages were left completely at the mercy of these lawless, and ruthless, gangs. [26]

KINGSTON BUCI

Less isolated than it used to be, Kingston is still quiet compared with the bustle of Piccadilly Circus. And yet there is a connection. Under the south window in the chancel is a plate in memory of Rev. Walter O. Purton, BA, who was rector here from 1870 to 1888 (he died in 1892 at the early age of 58). Earlier in his life he had been personal chaplain to the seventh Earl of Shaftesbury, the Victorian philanthropist; and Sir Alfred Gilbert's 'Eros' in Piccadilly Circus was erected as a memorial to Shaftesbury.

On the west side of Kingston Lane is a house called Ashcroft, now used as a training centre for the Central Electricity Generating Board. It belonged for some time to the Gorringe family and was then bought and lived in by the comedian Max Miller, the 'Cheeky Chappie'. [20]

KIRDFORD

Just on your left, a few yards inside the gate to Kirdford churchyard, is a remarkable tombstone, recording the deaths of seven people in three separate accidents within the space of twelve weeks. Edward Evershed, aged 37, died on January 5, 1838, from a fall from a horse, and Thomas Eames, aged 14, died on March 26 in the same year from being run over by a farm cart. In between occurred the puzzling tragedy of five teenage youths who came from four families. The tombstone records:

TO THE MEMORY OF
GEORGE NEWMAN aged 17
CHARLES NEWMAN aged 13
THOMAS RAPLEY aged 14
GEORGE PUTTICK aged 13
and WILLIAM BOXALL aged 19 years
who died at Sladeland on the 21st January 1838
from having placed green-wood ashes in their bedroom

One would like to know what happened. Did the ashes suffocate them? Were they in bed and asleep at the time? And why were they all in one bedroom together? Or did they die from quite a different cause, while superstition put the blame on the wood-ash which couldn't speak for itself? [9]

LANCING

Oscar Wilde's lover, and the central figure in the scandal which caused his downfall, Lord Alfred Douglas ('Bosie') died at Monks Farmhouse — home of Lancing's resident Roman Catholic priest.

The famous barrister Dr Kenealy spent his last 18 months at the Terrace, overlooking Beach Green. He's buried in a handsome tomb in Hangleton churchyard and features in the Willett Collection of terracotta at Brighton Museum, which shows characters in the Tichborne Claimant trial as animals. In 1854 Roger Tichborne, heir presumptive to considerable estates, sailed from Rio de Janeiro in a ship which was lost at sea. Kenealy unsuccessfully defended Arthur Orton who had tried to pass himself off as Tichborne. Orton was imprisoned for perjury.

Anna Sewell, author of that perennial favourite *Black Beauty*, lived in the village during her twenties. Here she had her first pony and trap, in which she would drive her father to the railway station at Shoreham.   [19]

LAUGHTON

The medieval love of relics now seems almost ludicrous: if they were all genuine, John the Baptist must have had at least four heads! The de Veres, Earls of Oxford, lived here for years, and in 1370 Thomas de Vere left his wife Maude, in his will, 'all his reliques then in his proper custody, with a certain cross made of the very wood of Christ's cross'.

Another considerable family were the de la Chambres, who had their original home at Chambers Court in Laughton — a place which no longer exists. One of the family is listed as having been among the 'happy few' at Agincourt. Later they moved to Litlington (where they built another Chambers Court, again vanished), and after that to Rodmell, Denton and Seaford.

But the great family here was, of course, that of the Pelhams (see *Introduction* and the *Laughton* and *Halland* entries in *Hidden Sussex*). Laughton Tower, hidden away down a long and winding farm track, is all that remains of their original home.   [22]

LAVANT

The Rev. Richard Batsworth, or Bettesworth, was rector of East Lavant from 1653 to 1657, and an extraordinary man he must have been. He's recorded as being 'a man of low stature, very violent for the rebels, and a plunderer of the royalists..... He had some learning, and a great deal of chicanery, though seldom more than one coat, which for some time he wore the wrong side out (its right side was only seen on Sundays) till it was almost worn out...'   [17]

LIDSEY

The monks at Aldingbourne before the Conquest built a chapel here. The very early Saxon font from the chapel now stands in Aldingbourne church (see illustration on page 20).   [17]

LINCH

In compiling a book such as this, curious coincidences are bound to occur. At the top of this page is Richard Bettesworth: for Linch we located another Bettesworth family — or perhaps they were related. Peter Bettesworth in the late 18th century was owner of several manors in West Sussex: we might have used the name under at least half-a-dozen headings. In his time the local chapel, an ancient building dedicated to St. Luke, was very dilapidated. Our Peter Bettesworth paid for the building of a new chapel on Woodman's Green, where his name and the date appear over the entrance door.

An earlier (Sir) Peter Bettesworth in the 1620s had owned the advowsons of Iping and Chithurst, as well as Iping Manor.

The village was a centre of the Sussex iron industry as long ago as the fourteenth century. A record dated 1342 shows that in that year the rector received ten shillings for the tithe of iron ore — one of the earliest examples of such a tithe from anywhere in the country, since tithes were normally taken from agricultural produce.   [8]

LINCHMERE

An oval plaque in the churchyard wall records that here is buried Richard Dimbleby, one of the best-loved of all radio and TV personalities, who is best remembered for the many royal ceremonials he described with calm fluency.   [1]

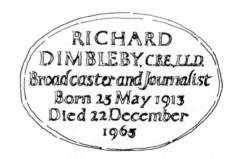

RICHARD DIMBLEBY, CBE, LLD.
Broadcaster and Journalist
Born 25 May 1913
Died 22 December 1965

LINDFIELD

The house Kennards was the seat of the Chaloner family, among them the Major Chaloner who was a supporter of Oliver Cromwell and an influential magistrate, and — on the other side of the divide altogether — Richard Chaloner (1691-1781), who was a leading Roman Catholic at a time when such a faith was highly unpopular.

Charles B. Cochran, the pre-war showman, was born here in 1872. He mounted a great many West End spectaculars including The Miracle and Cavalcade.

The founder of the Shaw, Savill shipping line, Walter Savill, lived at Finches. He died at the age of 76 in 1911 — and the very next day his 80-year-old brother died at Brighton.

One of the most remarkable athletes ever known was vicar here from 1929 until 1937. The Rev. Sidney Swann rowed three times for Cambridge in the Boat Race, rowed the English Channel in under four hours, was the first man to cycle round Syria and cycled from Carlisle to London in a day. He was also a hurdler, pole vaulter, swimmer, hammer thrower and weight putter. [11]

LITLINGTON

Clapham House was by tradition the home of Mrs Fitzherbert before George IV married her — and then discarded her. It's said that he used to ride from Brighton to see her. The village guide says 'this is quite probable, as Brighton is only 18 miles away', though we wonder whether George's stamina was equal to regular journeys of that kind. What seems in little doubt is that, despite his behaviour as Prince Regent and King, George loved Maria Fitzherbert as he did no other woman.

A later resident of Clapham House was Charles La Trobe, the first governor of Victoria, Australia. He died in the village in 1875. [28]

LITTLE COMMON

A 'tramp' who publishes an edition of poems, 600 copies 'on toned antique laid paper, and twenty upon hand-made paper' is undoubtedly an unusual character. Rupert Croft-Cooke published his *Songs of a Sussex Tramp* in 1922 (The Vine Press, Steyning). He came from St Leonards but his poems are set in various parts of the county. The dedication is suitably fey: 'These Reveries of the Road I Dedicate to COSMO, who has been with me on Foot in Sussex, and on Dream Ships through the World.' It was the moon shining on the damp road at Little Common as Croft-Cooke walked to Bexhill that inspired the poem 'God's Own':

> There is poetry abroad tonight;
> The moon makes merry with the earth:
> Like the laughing of the children is her light —
> Like God's Own children's mirth [24]

LITTLE HORSTED

In the course of a nineteenth-century restoration of the church six odd pieces of stone were found in use as building material. They fitted together exactly, and showed that the whole stone had been inscribed as a memorial to some otherwise unknown member of the family of Delve in 1502. A later generation produced one Thomas Delve who in 1542 made a will leaving 'to the High Altar of Horsestede for tithes forgotten vi^d.' and the remarkable 'to each of my grandchildren, if they ask for it, iiij^d.' In those days fourpence was worth it.   [12/21]

LITTLEWORTH

At Jolesfield in this parish there used to be a smock mill built in, or just before, 1788. It became derelict in about 1928 and remained so until 1959. It then belonged to Mr Nevvar Hickmet, who had recently acquired Gatwick Manor restaurant. He planned to move the entire mill to the Gatwick Manor site as an attraction, but this proved impracticable, and although the machinery went, the brick base stayed put at Littleworth and was converted into a stable. Having got the works to Gatwick, Mr. Hickmet seemed to lose interest in his uncompleted scheme, and the great wood and iron parts slowly decayed from exposure to wind and rain.   [11]

LODSWORTH

Though apparently not a man of Sussex, Mr. A.E. Bass claims a mention in these pages. He designed a striking modern stained glass window in the porch here, depicting St. Nicholas, the fourth century bishop of Myra and now the patron saint of children — the original Santa Claus, a corruption of Santo Nicholaos. Bass also designed the huge rose window at Lancing College which was dedicated in 1981.   [9]

LORDINGTON

The house was built in the late 15th century by Sir Richard Pole, KG, later Earl of Salisbury. His treacherous second son, Geoffrey, married Margaret, daughter of that Duke of Clarence who, as Shakespeare tells and every schoolboy knows, was drowned in a butt of Malmsey wine. Geoffrey commanded a company against the rebels in the Pilgrimage of Grace, intending to desert his troops and join the rebels if necessary. Then he joined with Lord Exeter and others to organize a rising in the West Country. When danger threatened he scurried to London and gave evidence to the Privy Council about the rising, getting a pardon for himself while his ex-comrades were beheaded.

Sir Richard's fourth son Reginald became the great cardinal and last Roman Catholic archbishop of Canterbury. He studied at Padua and after an adventurous life Pope Paul III sent him back to England as papal legate; he died in 1558.   [30]

LOWER BEEDING

In the 16th century Thomas Lord Seymour owned considerable areas of land around Lower Beeding in St Leonard's Forest, and he had the bright idea, four centuries before the Crawley experience, of building a new town on his land. Detailed plans were drawn up, but Thomas had too many irons in the fire: himself Lord High Admiral of England, he was discovered to be plotting against his brother, the Protector of the young Edward VI. A bloody end was put to his career and 'Seymourtown' never got beyond the drawing-board.

There was a persistent story of a monster here, which may have got confused with the one St Leonard destroyed. Be that as it may, in the 17th century 'the Horsham carrier and other three' actually clapped eyes on the beast, which they said 'cast his venom four rods'. Its principal food was the rabbits of the neighbouring warren and it measured nine feet in length with bunches at the sides that the carrier and his friends feared might at any moment turn into wings. Unfortunately the records don't say anything about the state of the weather or of the sobriety of the viewers.   [11]

LOWER DICKER

Who the first Dickers were is a matter of dispute. William Berry, in his *Sussex Genealogies*, says that Nicholas Dicker from a place called Rotherfield Pipard in Oxfordshire was the ancestor of the Sussex family, but Mark Anthony Lower says that one William at Dicker in fact took his name from the district. And what of the coat of arms? It's officially described as 'Argent, on a chevron gules, between three Cornish choughs proper, a crescent Or'. Choughs are members of the crow family and there seems no obvious reason for their inclusion, but the heraldic authority Dr L.F. Salzman has put forward the idea that they're an example of canting, or punning: 'One feels that the birds were not intended to be choughs, but just "dickie-birds"'!   [22]

LOWFIELD HEATH

Two brothers, Henry and John Cheal, were born here about 150 years ago. Henry became a builder; John, a Quaker, started up as a shopkeeper in the little village of Crawley, and then as a small farmer in Lowfield Heath. In 1871 his two sons, Joseph and Alexander, began to grow trees, and John joined in the scheme, to found Cheal's Nurseries. Two of Joseph's children, Ernest and Arthur, entered the business. Very many years later Ernest, as an old man, assisted our present Queen and the Duke of Edinburgh when they planted trees from Cheal's to mark the opening of Gatwick Airport and the new Queen's Square in Crawley. The company was later to pass out of the family's hands, but it still carries the name: it's now situated at Stopham.   [4]

LOXWOOD

John Sirgood was a shoemaker-preacher who, divinely guided in a dream, came to Sussex from London in 1850 and began to preach from his own cottage in Loxwood. The antinomian doctrine of his Society of Dependants (see *Hidden Sussex*) declared that true members of the sect could do no wrong, a privileged position reflected in one of their hymns:

> *Though in this world we take our place,*
> *As other mortals do,*
> *We're all imbued by Him with grace*
> *And he will see us through.*
> *He will know his sparkling jewels*
> *Those in whom His image shines,*
> *He will spare us and preserve us,*
> *He will say, Yes these are mine.* [2]

LULLINGTON

In the time of Elizabeth I the lord of the manor was the great poet Sir Philip Sidney, who died in 1586 in Holland, aged only 32. His literary output was enormous when you consider that he was much engaged as a courtier and as a diplomat in France, Italy, Hungary, Germany and the Netherlands. His sonnet sequence *Astrophel and Stella* contains some of the loveliest lyrics in the English language.

The dedication of the church is unknown, but Jegelian Hunt (what marvellously ingenious Christian names our forbears thought up for their offspring: although see *Hadlow Down*!) in his will of 1521 left a bequest to the high altar and also 'a taper to be set before St Sithe'. It's uncertain who this saint was — possibly the martyred Saxon princess whom we know as St Osyth, but more likely St Zita or Sitha, the 13th century virgin maidservant of Lucca in Tuscany, who by her virtues has become the patron saint of all domestic workers. Her feast day is April 27. [28]

LURGASHALL

Before organs became almost an essential feature of church furnishing, a small band led the singing. In 1639 Robert Jennance, a band musician, left in his will 'my bass vyolin to Edward Tupper, my zitterne to Henry Challin, my trible vyolin to Robert Wilkinson'. George Sadler was the mainstay of the last band here. On the Sunday after his death in 1838 the band broke down and was 'niver no sense arterwards'. [9]

LYMINSTER

The manor was bequeathed by King Alfred in his will to his nephew Osferd, so it must have been a considerable place. It possessed a nunnery in Saxon times and later a small priory of Augustinian nuns. Shortly before the Conquest one Suane, son of Godwin Earl of Kent, inveigled the abbess Edwina with intent to marry her. It takes two to make a marriage, however, and Edwina must surely have been guilty of a little un-nunlike conduct. [18]

MADEHURST

Mowbray (he seems to have had no other name, though he was known even more simply as Mo) was a shepherd in the service of a local farmer, Jack Adames. Mo had been a farmer on his own until he struck hard times and was glad to be taken on as shepherd and foreman. He loved his sheep, as is recorded in Gerard Young's *The Cottage in the Fields*. One summer evening Mr Adames witnessed a remarkable spectacle: 'I was walking through the woods and I came out above the great hollow we called Valley Field. It was just on sunset and right down below me I saw old Mo. He was standing there, leaning on a stick, and was completely surrounded by a great circle of sheep, all with their faces turned in towards him. There was absolute stillness and I watched Mo turning slowly and looking at each individual sheep. He knew them all and was just contentedly saying goodnight to them. It was like a beautiful picture out of the Bible.' [18]

MARDENS The

North, East, West and Up have known several interesting inhabitants, among them Earl Russell, who was Minister of Transport during the first world war and who lived at Telegraph House in North Marden. His more famous philosopher brother, Lord Bertrand Russell, started the school Battine House at East Marden around 1928 and later moved it to North Marden. Russell had forceful views about intellectual and other freedoms for school children.

Two sporting connections: Brigadier Critchley, one of the originators of greyhound racing, lived at Manor House, East Marden. Students of cricket history will know the name of Lamborn, demon bowler of the original Hambledon XI. He lived at Up Marden. [17/29]

MARESFIELD

Thomasine Edwards must have fancied her chances of a long and successful marriage when, in Puritan times, she wed Performe-thy-Vowes Seers of Maresfield. The Puritans showed great resourcefulness in raiding Biblical texts for their children's names, though the results weren't always happy. An itinerant tinker is said to have called his son 'Alas', having misunderstood the text (I Kings ch 13 v 30) '....and they mourned over him, saying, Alas, my brother'. We must register the feeling, however, that this tale may be apocryphal!

Richard Bonner was rector here in the late 17th century and was buried in the chancel of the church in 1692. He founded a school which still flourishes as Bonner's Church of England Primary School after nearly 300 years. He also left money in trust for a 'Bonner's Bible' annual award to the pupil showing most 'industrie and diligence'. [12]

101

MARK CROSS

A local yeoman named Bridger must have been a bit of an oddity. He was extremely tall, with fiery red hair plaited into a pigtail which he kept tied halfway down his back with a white satin ribbon: and he took little trouble about his dress. Yet he was a kindly and generous man, who had a large estate with a lodge in which he allowed tramps to sleep. One day a local policeman (a newcomer to the district, he must have been) saw a ragged creature crouched over a fire of sticks near the lodge, took him into custody and marched him off to Mark Cross, where the magistrates were sitting. To their surprise, the offender was found to be none other than Bridger himself. Rearing himself to full height, he told the policeman: 'I'll trouble you not to come interfering on *my* land in future.'   [**13**]

MAYFIELD

After the Old Palace ceased to be an ecclesiastical residence (see *Hidden Sussex*) it was sold off, and in 1567 Sir Thomas Gresham, founder of the Royal Exchange, bought the property. His sign was a grasshopper and several adorn the chimney, dated 1571, of 'Queen Elizabeth's chamber'. The name reflects the fact that the Virgin Queen stayed here in 1573.

Gabriel Tomkins was leader of the Mayfield Gang, notorious smugglers and felons in the 18th century. A bricklayer from Tunbridge Wells, he was also known as Kitt Jarvis, Joseph Rawlins and Unkle. Although between 1717 and 1729 he was tried for murdering a customs officer and acquitted, sentenced to transportation (he talked his way to freedom by informing) and recaptured for persistent smuggling, he was by 1735 actually appointed a customs officer himself and bailiff to the Sheriff of Sussex! This was not a case of the repentant sinner, as he was hanged in 1750 for robbing the Chester Mail.

The 19th century sculptor Sir Thomas Brook, who's buried in the churchyard, engraved the portrait of Queen Victoria which was used on coins during the latter part of her life. His initials appear on them.

C.B. Fry, the great all-round sportsman and cricket captain of Sussex and England, came from an old Mayfield family. The Mayfield Cricket Club is now well over a hundred years old and has, in the past, proved itself quite able to stand up to distinguished touring and county sides. In 1912 Kirby and Marwick put up a first wicket partnership of no less than 324 runs against Tunbridge Wells — a record, so far as we can ascertain, still unbeaten. Kirby was the son of the then vicar of Mayfield, and thereby hangs another record: between 1780 and 1912 there were four vicars from the same family.   [**13**]

MERSTON

This small former parish (718 acres only) and its manor have known good times and bad. Henry fitz Roger held the manor in 1344. He had two sons, one of whom picked a great quarrel with their neighbours, Sir Thomas and Maude de Holand. This almost turned into a feud and must have disrupted the whole district, but happily they all made it up in 1346 — so much so that the de Holands stood as godfathers to Thomas fitz Roger, in days when standing as godparents really involved some responsibility. Less lucky was Lord Bonvyle, who held the manor in the next century. He was beheaded on February 19, 1461, after the second battle of St Albans when, as a Lancastrian, he was taken prisoner by the warlike Yorkist Margaret of Anjou, queen of Henry VI. His heir was his great-granddaughter Cecily, then only nine months old. When she grew up she married Thomas Grey, son of Edward IV's queen Elizabeth, and the manor of Merston was settled on the happy couple.   [25]

MIDDLETON

We tell something of Charlotte Smith under *Bignor*. She visited Middleton, then almost deserted, and the loneliness of the place stirred her Muse (as she herself might have put it). She described it as 'a village on the margin of the sea, containing only two or three houses. There were formerly several acres of ground between its small church and the sea, which now, by its continual encroachment, approaches within a few feet of this half-ruined and humble edifice. The wall, which once surrounded the churchyard, is entirely swept away, many of the graves broken up, and the remains of bodies interred washed into the sea.' She wrote a very melancholy sonnet, from which we give four lines:

> *The wild blast, rising from the western cave,*
> *Drives the huge billows from their heaving bed;*
> *Tears from their grassy tombs the village dead,*
> *And breaks the silent sabbath of the grave!*   [26]

MIDHURST

Charles James Fox became MP for Midhurst in 1768 at the tender age of 19, but although he was a leading political figure until his death in 1806 he never led his Whig party to power (unless we count the brief coalition of 1783). The historian G. M. Trevelyan described him as the eternal schoolboy: 'Devoted to his friends; generous to his enemies but always up in arms against them for any reason or none; never out of scrapes; a lover of life and of mankind, he was born to be leader of opposition, and leader of opposition he was for almost all his long life in the House of Commons.'

A far less illustrious character was William Edwards who, in April 1791, 'having been drunk for two days', undertook to drink 18 glasses of gin on the condition that other people should pay for them. He managed to sink 17½, after which he was carried off to a nearby hovel where he died.   [8]

MILLAND

Notable visitors to Milland Place in the years before the first world war were the kings of Norway, Denmark and Sweden, the young Winston Churchill and even the German Emperor Wilhelm the Second ('Kaiser Bill'): he's said to have made good use of the historic real tennis court. Their hostess was the Viscountess Massereene & Ferrard, still remembered locally for her large hats and her beautifully turned out black landau drawn by two coal black horses, with a coachman and two footmen in full livery.

There are those who believe that Hugh Gaitskell would have made one of our great Prime Ministers had death not struck him down at a comparatively young age. At one time he'd almost decided to take up an academic career, but during a walk in the Milland valley with Hugh Dalton he was persuaded instead to enter politics. He owned a small farm here for a time and always had an affection for the area. He returned to open the original village hall.

Thomas Otway the dramatist was born at the rectory here in 1682. (See *Trotton*).   [1]

MILTON STREET

The surname Ade isn't common, but a family so called lived at the old manor house, Milton Court, for well over two centuries. The most outstanding member was Charles Ade, a well-known archaeologist and coin collector. He contributed a learned article on Anglo-Saxon coins to the very first number of the *Sussex Archaeological Collections* in 1848.   [28]

MONK'S GATE

The composer Ralph Vaughan Williams travelled all over England collecting the tunes and words of old folksongs, and he was the compiler and editor of the first edition of *The English Hymnal*, published in 1906. He was not a Sussex man; he was born in Gloucestershire and finished his life near Dorking in Surrey. In his earlier years he had been a protagonist of the movement to revive English folksong, and for the *Hymnal* he wrote four new tunes himself besides arranging nearly sixty others. His practice was to name tunes after the place where they were collected. At Monk's Gate a Mrs Harriet Verrall sang to him 'Our Captain Calls'. Vaughan Williams adapted the tune to the words 'He who would valiant be, 'gainst all disaster' and named it Monk's Gate. The hymnal contains other tunes named Rodmell, Lodsworth, Horsham, Rusper and Kingsfold, but the melody of Monk's Gate echoed in Vaughan Williams' head and later in his life it matured in his great opera *The Pilgrim's Progress*.   [5]

MOUNTFIELD

Readers who have hard memories of their classroom days will feel for young Ernest Jenner, victim of schoolmasterish sarcasm in the records for 1904 of Sedlescombe school:

July 6. Ernest Jenner admitted from Mountfield School.
July 7. Ernest Jenner was so convinced of the fact that we work
        here that he returned to Mountfield School.

We record here a most remarkable coincidence. Some years ago the Massey Ferguson Tractor Co. were seeking a church situated above a sloping field for an advertisement photograph. After viewing scores of churches all over England they found their ideal at Mountfield. Imagine their astonishment on finding, in the stained glass east window, a picture of an identical tractor, of whose existence they were quite unaware! [14]

MUDDLES GREEN

Mark Antony Lower, the great name among Sussex historians, was born here in 1813; he died in 1876 after a life devoted to collecting source material for the county. A pioneer member of the Sussex Archaeological Society, he wrote several books on aspects of Sussex, besides a strange compilation entitled *Contributions to Literature* (1854) which included essays on place names, the Battle of Hastings, ironworks, yew trees in churchyards and genealogy, besides several mock ballads, all showing the range of his enthusiasms. [22]

MUNDHAM

It's on record that Queen Elizabeth I visited here, though not whether she slept. On December 8, 1588, she attended a service of thanksgiving for victory over the Spanish Armada.

The house Leythorn was built by Robert Sherburn, bishop of Chichester, in the 16th century. It gradually slid down until by about 1750 it was a mere farmhouse. Then along from Chichester came a Mr. Newland, who bought the house and made of it a factory for weaving broadcloth. The planners would have something to say about such a scheme today! Unluckily, the venture was a disaster, and the building fell into decay and was demolished in 1798. [25]

MUNTHAM

See *Findon*.

NEPCOTE

The Nepcote fair, unlike some we record, is almost new — a mere couple of centuries old. By the early 1900s it was large enough to attract nationwide interest. The auctioneer in those days was H.J. Burt of Steyning, whose name (now incorporated in Churchman, Burt & Son) is still associated with the fair on September 14, held for many years for pleasure as well as business.

In the 19th century Nepcote was a centre of religious nonconformity, giving space to Mormons, Baptists, Plymouth Brethren, Independents and others. Such activity must have been quite rare for a hamlet with only about 100 souls.

[19]

NETHERFIELD

Clerical ironmasters are rare even in Sussex, but here there is a record of Rev. John Gyles. He acquired the Ashburnham forge in 1640 and in 1649 he was granted a licence to take earth for making and repairing bays in the Netherfield area. On his death in 1654 he left his share in extensive ironworkings to his wife Joane, who married in succession four ironmasters. Gyles' partner in the trade was his nephew Benjamin Scarlett, whose sons in 1667 entered into a complicated legal document regarding water supplies and furnaces at Netherfield.

[14]

NEWBRIDGE

In the days before registration of births and christenings, how did you prove your date of birth so that, for instance, you could come into an inheritance? In 1372 William de L'Isle had to do that in this small hamlet close to Pulborough. You brought before the magistrates or law officers all the people you could muster who could testify to some incident which would help fix it. William's 'team' included four people who remembered that they had married in that year (1350); one had a son born in that year; three said that they had accompanied the Countess of Ormond who had arrived at her husband's house on the day of William's birth; and three others recalled that one Richard Somere had bought a house and garden at Billingshurst and had moved in on the very day William was born. There's a good handful of circumstantial stories!

[10]

NEWICK

Perhaps the most unusual death we have come across befell John Boots in May 1737. He was playing cricket at Newick and, according to the parish register, was killed 'by running against another man on crossing wicket.'

At Beechlands lived William Henry Blaauw (1793-1870). A member of many learned societies including the Society of Antiquaries, he was a prime mover of the Sussex Archaeological Society; on its formation on June 18, 1846 he was elected the first Hon. Secretary and sole Editor of the Collections — offices he held for eight years. He was the chief research archaeologist into the remains of Earl Warenne and Lady Gundrada (see *Southover*).

[12]

NEWTIMBER

In 1902 Sydney Buxton and his wife Mildred moved into Newtimber Place. They'd been married for seven years and Sydney was a rising Liberal politician. In the Liberal landslide of 1906 he was made Postmaster General with a seat in the Cabinet.In 1914 he was given a peerage and the GCMG and was sent to South Africa as Governor General, a post he held for six years. After her husband's death in 1934 Lady Buxton kept the house going and established a reputation as a hostess, besides her untiring public work. She was awarded the CBE and died in 1955 at the grand age of 89.   [20]

NINFIELD

The best-known example of wife-selling occurs in *The Mayor of Caster-bridge* but the phenomenon wasn't unknown in real life, and several instances have been recorded in Sussex. At Ninfield stocks (pictured in *Hidden Sussex*) a wife was sold for half a pint of gin in 1790. She was delivered in the traditional way, with a halter about her neck in the presence of two witnesses. A contemporary account recorded that 'she appeared mightily delighted about the ceremony, and the hopeful pair departed filled with joy and expectation from the happy union.'

The beginnings of the Salvation Army can, without too much manipulation of events, be traced to Ninfield. In 1871 the freelance evangelist William Booth gave the opening sermon when his friend William Corbridge launched his so-called Christian Mission in the village. Booth was later to adopt this name for his own similar churches until, in 1878, he hit on the title The Salvation Army. Booth's signature, incidentally, is in the Ninfield parish records: he was a witness when Corbridge registered his daughter's birth.   [23]

NORTHCHAPEL

A lady whom we know only as Mrs Blackwell must have been a character. She's named as having been mistress of an iron forge and furnace here. Ernest Straker, in his book *Wealden Iron,* noted that she was 'an outwardly conforming but much suspected recusant, and her house in London at Blackfriars (which at a later date was purchased by Shakespeare as an investment) was a noted hiding-place for priests. As it was closely watched, her successors there refused admission to the Gunpowder Plot conspirators.' The furnace at Northchapel was worked well into the 18th century.

Northchapel was made a separate parish in 1718 and, remarkably, had only two rectors from that date until 1816. The first was Samuel Meymott, whose meticulously kept register has a number of interesting entries, such as: 'Aug. 14, 1726. Ann, a negro belonging to Mr Glanvile, of St John's Town in Antegoa, was baptized by me, Samuel Meynott.' The second rector, Dr Colin Milne, never lived in the parish at all. He compiled a pioneer botanical dictionary, published 1770.   [2]

NORTHEYE

The land around Pevensey Levels needed constant attention in the Middle Ages, and a number of drainage documents have survived. In 1289 King Edward I appointed Luke de la Gare one of the Conservators of Pevensey Marsh. But Luke raised up a bank and sluice across the haven, with the result that instead of draining the marsh he drowned it. The landowners whose acres were inundated included the Abbot of Battle and the Prior of Lewes, both of whom made strong complaint to the king. He appointed a commission of inquiry which inspected the damage and eventually had the impediment removed. One of the commission members was William de Northeye, clearly a local man, probably with local knowledge.

Northeye was for many years a 'limb' of the Cinque Port of Hastings, but it was deserted and the village is now merely an area of bumps and hollows.

[23]

NORTH HEATH

Often in times long past a convict sentenced to death would be executed in the local gaol, and then his body would be hung on a gibbet at the scene of his crime as a dire warning to others. To make the lesson more terrible, his body would be left in chains until it rotted or was blown away by the wind. One of the very last instances of this gruesome procedure was in the case of the two Drewitt brothers, convicted in 1799 of robbing the Portsmouth mail coach on North Heath Common. After execution at Horsham they were strung up at North Heath. But the query arose whether the younger of them was guilty at all. It was long believed in the area that he was innocent, but could not prove it without implicating his father, the real culprit; so rather than betray his parent he went to the gallows.

[10]

NORTHIAM

Nathaniel Lloyd was one of the most erudite writers on the *History of the English House*. His book with that title was published in 1931, rapidly established itself and is now a classic. He lived for many years at the famed Great Dixter, a medieval house which he largely preserved and restored. Now no book on architecture would be complete without a picture of it.

Much earlier, Northiam had been the home of the Frewen family who came to Sussex in 1583. Rector John Frewen's Puritan sympathies induced him to name his first son (born 1588) Accepted, his second (b. 1591) Thankfull. After that his choice became more usual, with names such as John and Joseph. Accepted Frewen followed a very brilliant academic career culminating in his becoming Archbishop of York in 1660, the year of the Restoration.

The novelist Sheila Kaye-Smith, best known for *Joanna Godden*, lived at the oddly-named Little Doucegrove. She wrote over fifty books, including several about Sussex.

[15]

NUTBOURNE

The Mille family were well established in the Pulborough district of Sussex by the fourteenth century, and lived at Mille Place. Although of yeoman stock, they were staunch Royalists and became connected by marriage with the Lewknors, Challoners, Gorings and other eminent county families. They even aspired to a family vault, which stood for three centuries in the south-west corner of Pulborough churchyard. Then in the 17th century it was demolished, and two brasses from it, though in poor condition, were taken into the church, where they still are.   [10]

NUTHURST

We came across an odd example of the relative values of money. In the reign of Charles I, a monarch always short of cash, a local yeoman named Thomas Patching was able to compound for a knighthood at the modest sum of £10. A few years later, during the Commonwealth, another Nuthurst man, William Pierce was mulcted in the sum of £465. 7s. 8d. for having Royalist sympathies. Any supporter of the exiled king was liable to persecution; the rector here in 1643 was George Edgeley, DD, described later as "a person that hath expressed his loyalty by his active services and passive sufferings for the defence of His Majesty's person, religion and laws."   [10]

NUTLEY

Thomas Henslowe was Master of Ashdown Forest under Queen Mary Tudor. He was a pretty unscrupulous character only concerned for his own enrichment. He got rid of the Forest's honest officials one by one, in favour of his paid henchmen who quelled by violence any criticism of his abuses. He regularly engaged in illegal sales of forest timber and livestock, to such an extent that eventually the commoners made direct complaint to the Queen. Despite Henslowe's counter-accusations of nighttime poaching by royal tenants and others, it seems he was at last removed from office. He is not heard of after 1559, by which time Queen Elizabeth I was on the throne.   [12]

NYEWOOD

Thanks to the *The Natural History of Selborne*, Gilbert White, probably our most famous naturalist after Darwin, is usually connected more with Hampshire than with Sussex. But for almost forty years (1754-1792) White was an East Harting squire. The bulk of his estate was at Woodhouse and here at Nyewood — formerly Nye Woods — and he spent much of his time in the area.   [8/29]

OFFHAM

Simon de Montfort was, in the words of the historian G. M. Trevelyan, 'one of those commanding natures, like Cromwell or Chatham, who cannot play the second part'. This dominating personality brought bloodshed to Sussex on May 14, 1264, when Henry III's army was defeated at the Battle of Lewes. De Montfort's army occupied Fletching and Piltdown commons

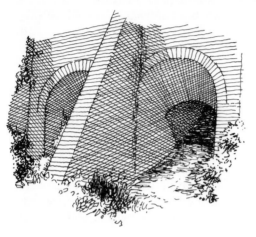

before the battle, and many a village and hamlet must have been affected by the ensuing carnage, but it was upon Offham Hill that the rebel army gathered — trapping the royalists in the town.

In *Hidden Sussex* we mention the inclined plane which took trucks from the chalk pits down the steep slope to the River Ouse. A Lewes schoolmaster named Cater Rand is recorded as the designer and planner of the project, but we've been unable to discover what qualifications he had for the job.   **[21]**

ORE

The French Jesuit priest Pierre Teilhard de Chardin — who became famous for his archaeological research and scientific discoveries after the first world war, and who developed some highly controversial evolutionary theories — completed his theological training at Ore. He was poking about a gravel pit near the college when he met the amateur archaeologist Charles Dawson, who was later to involve him in the discovery of Piltdown Man (see *Piltdown* in *Hidden Sussex*). When, 40 years afterwards, the affair was exposed as a hoax, Teilhard was deeply wounded. 'I still have trouble,' he wrote, 'believing that Dawson himself perpetrated the fraud.'   **[24]**

OTHAM

A charter from the small Premonstratensian monastery here reveals that peat was regularly dug in the 12th century: it's all been used up long since. The charter details the work expected from the villein Hugo de Dudintun, who 'is bound to carry manure for iij days; also to work one day in every fifteen...he is bound one day to mow grass, another to collect, and a third to bring to the stack. He is bound also for j day to cut bushes or heath wherever it may be appointed him; j day to carry the same....' The last of a series of Roman numeral i's was usually given a tail, so j is one, iij is three.   **[22]**

OVING

The tithes and prebendal manor of Oving belonged from early times to the precentor of Chichester Cathedral. In 1225 the precentor was Hugo de Talmaco, who handed over the tithes and some other income to the parish vicar. Included was an acre of land given to the church so that from its profits two wax tapers could be maintained lit in the church. The field was soon given the name 'Lamp Acre'. However, under Elizabeth I this kind of thing was considered superstitious by the Protestants, and the field was confiscated by the Crown.   [17]

OVINGDEAN

In *Hidden Sussex* we gave five lines to Magnus Volk. He deserves more. His family came from the Black Forest area of Germany, but he was born in Brighton in 1851, his father being a clockmaker in Western Road. By the time he was twenty he was turning his mind to all kinds of scientific invention, to such effect that he is worthy of being dubbed the English Edison. Among his achievements were a 'parlour telegraph' for domestic communication; fire alarms; remote detonators for under-water mines; a pipe organ; and even a seaplane station during World War I. But his name will always be best remembered in connection with the Brighton Seafront Railway. He died in 1937 and, as he had requested, is buried in Ovingdean churchyard.   [21]

PAGHAM

According to Bede, in 687 King Ceadwalla of the South Saxons gave much of the land in this region to St. Wilfrid in penance for the devastation he had caused during the fight for his kingdom. To demonstrate his sorrow, he resigned his crown and went as a pilgrim to Rome.

Another Sussex saint is associated with Pagham. In 1242 Friar Humphrey, the recluse of Pagham, was among five anchorites who were bequeathed sums of money under the will of no less a person than St. Richard de Wyche.

The parish church is dedicated to St. Thomas à Becket, and may be one of the very earliest so offered. Becket was murdered on December 29, 1170, and was canonized three years later. His successor in the archbishopric was Richard of Dover, who came to Pagham in 1179 and by 1204 was granted by King John the right to hold a market and fair here, mentioning the church's dedication by name. But this is not the first church on the site: an archaeological 'dig' in 1976 revealed remains not only of a Norman church but of a Saxon one as well. People have lived here for well over a thousand years.   [25]

PARHAM

The manor came to the family of Bisshopp of Henfield in 1597; the baronetcy was created in 1620, and the eighth in the line was made Baron Zouche in 1815. His daughter and heiress, Harriet-Anne Bisshopp, married into the family of the Viscounts Curzon. Robert Curzon, the fourteenth Baron Zouche (1810-1873) was an antiquarian and traveller of a most rare kind. Among other books, he wrote *Visits to the Monasteries of the Levant*, in which he tells of his adventures in search of antiquities, especially ancient manuscripts, in Egypt, Jerusalem, Meteora and Mount Athos. It was published in 1849, and after well over 130 years remains one of the most readable and exciting books of travel ever written. **[18/19]**

PATCHAM

The first Sussex author whose name has come down to us was John Peckham, or John of Patcham, since he was born here. He showed early promise enough to be taken in charge by the monks of St. Pancras Priory, Lewes, and he was taught by them. Determination and diplomacy eventually helped him to become Archbishop of Canterbury.

Here is buried Daniel Scales, who, according to his tombstone, was 'unfortunately shot on Thursday eve, 7th. November, 1796.' Then follow eight lines of sorrowing verse, of which the last four are:

> *'All ye who do this stone draw near,*
> *Oh! Pray let fall the pitying tear.*
> *From the sad instance may we all*
> *Prepare to meet Jehovah's call.'*

From this you might infer that poor Daniel was the victim of a tragic accident. But no: he was the leader of a notorious gang of smugglers, and he was killed by a mounted officer as the gang was trying to get away from Brighton with a heavy load of contraband. **[20]**

PATCHING

Truffles used to be considered a great delicacy. They are a fungus (*Tuber aestivum* and other varieties) growing below the surface under beech and similar trees, and pigs and dogs were specially trained to nose them out. In the late 18th century a man named William Leech came from the West Indies to Patching, where he set up as a truffle-hunter. He trained dogs for the purpose, and made a good living right until his death, a good few years later.

One Sunday in mid-Victorian times there came to church the family of a farmer, people who had risen a bit in the world, who drove their own carriage and affected 'style'. But evidently they had not learnt manners, as they chattered and giggled throughout the service. At last Sir John Kirkland, of nearby Dulaney House, walked across the aisle — in the middle of the service — and stood solemnly bowing at their pew until they shamefacedly left the church. **[19]**

PEACEHAVEN

The creator of Peacehaven, Charles Neville, was born in England but made his money overseas. He'd developed land in Canada and prospected for gold in New Guinea when, in the summer of 1914, he drove over the Downs from Newhaven in his American-made Hupmobile. Within ten years his South Coast Land and Resort Company owned a stretch of land five miles long by a mile wide. In 1916, through the national press, he advertised a competition to find a name for the emerging town, originally tagged Lureland. The first prize was £100 and the two joint winners chose Anzac on Sea in honour of the Australian and New Zealand Army Corps fighting in the first world war. When the Gallipoli expedition failed disastrously the name was changed to Peacehaven, the choice of over 200 entrants. It's said that more than 2,000 second prizes of plots of land were awarded to competitors, but they had to pay three guineas legal fees and some took Neville to court and got their money back. He died in 1960 at the age of 79.

When the Hotel Peacehaven was opened in 1922 the Dutch aircraft designer Anthony Fokker gave the country's first gliding display. There was some illfeeling when the Daily Mail tried to muscle in on the event, but the newspaper was eventually frustrated.

Other names connected with Peacehaven include the singer Gracie Fields, who founded an orphanage here (she lived at Telscombe Cliffs), and Felix Powell, who wrote songs such as 'Come to Peacehaven' and 'The Lureland Waltz' but is best known for 'Pack Up Your Troubles in Your Old Kit Bag'. [27]

PEASE POTTAGE

The first Baron Erskine, who lived here, ran a thriving business which made and supplied besom brooms for London and other towns. He wasn't long in being given the nickname 'the broom-dashing lord', but he was possessed of a fine legal mind and at one time had been no less a person than Lord High Chancellor of England.

PEASMARSH

In *Hidden Sussex* we mentioned the local poet William Pattison but had no room to tell how he began. M. A. Lower relates that while at school 'Pattison contracted debts to the amount of about ten pounds with some booksellers at Penrith. The creditors became very noisy in their demand, but the schoolboy poet had no money wherewith to satisfy them. What to do he did not know. At last he hit upon the happy expedient of writing himself out of debt. He penned an *Ode on Christmas Day,* and inscribed it to Sir Christopher Musgrave of Edenhall. He then introduced himself to the worthy baronet, who was so much delighted with the performance that he immediately directed his chaplain to pay the debts.' [15]

PENHURST

William Hobday, whose death was recorded by the rector of Penhurst in 1883, was the last surviving labourer of the last iron furnace to be worked in the county — at neighbouring Ashburnham. In *Hidden Sussex* we gave 1820 as the date at which it closed, though some records have suggested that it continued until 1828. Hobday, however, claimed that work stopped as early as 1813. He remembers that, as a boy, he had seen the last fire extinguished in that year. Three firebacks still in use at Penhurst manor house were, he said, the last ones to be cast there. 'Will Rummins cast them,' he added.   [14/23]

PETT

There's a puzzle about the bell in Pett church which is surely beyond hope of solution. On the chancel arch is a small brass with the charming inscription:

> *Here lies George Theobald a lover of Bells,*
> *And of this howse as that epitaph tells,*
> *He gave a bell freely to grace the new steple,*
> *Ring out his prayse therefore ye good people.*
> *Obit. 10mo die Martii Anno Dom. 1641*

There's only the one bell, and that certainly bears the date 1641, but the inscription on it is 'Robert Foster gave x^{1}v. toward me'.

The civil engineer who master-minded the early stages of the Royal Military Canal, which starts at Pett, was John Rennie. Unfortunately, he was a difficult man to deal with. He asserted that his job was the equivalent of a Field Marshal's — and he demanded a salary to match. Despite his undoubted abilities his temperament was his undoing, and he was sacked.   [24]

PETWORTH

One of those villages with so many associations that any entry will seem inadequate. Three great families have owned Petworth House during the span of more than 600 years — the Percys, the Seymours and the Wyndhams. Capability Brown designed the Park; the artists Turner and Constable both painted here (Constable finding the place too cold for his comfort); there are wood carvings by Grinling Gibbons.

We'd like, however, to mention one of the unknowns — Mary Boxall who, the parish register reveals, was certified on March 29, 1686, as having received 'His Maiesty's Sacred Touch'. The ancient custom of touching for the King's evil (scrofula, or tuberculosis) was initiated in England by Edward the Confessor and had a vogue after the Restoration.   [9]

114

PEVENSEY

One of the county's best ghost stories. Robert, Earl of Mortaigne, lord of the rape of Pevensey, was hunting in the forest near here on August 2, 1100 when he was confronted by 'a great and terrible black goat, which bore upon its back the semblance of the body of King (William) Rufus'. The earl challenged it, whereupon the apparition replied: 'I am carrying your king to judgement, yea, that tyrant William Rufus.' On that day, and at about that very hour, Rufus was killed in the New Forest.

We're aware that women make all too few appearances in our book, especially in affairs of State, so we're delighted to note an exception here. When John of Gaunt's son Henry, Duke of Lancaster, claimed the throne in 1399 Richard II laid siege to Pevensey Castle, which was one of his strongholds. Henry wasn't at home and neither was the castle's Constable, Sir John Pelham, so the defence was left in the hands of Sir John's wife, Lady Joan. The place was in sore need of repair, but the capable lady held the fort until the Duke's army arrived. Not surprisingly, Sir John was retained as Constable once his master became King Henry IV. Among the prisoners he held at Pevensey was the future James I of Scotland.

The Old Mint House was the home of Andrew Borde ('Merry Andrew': see *Introduction*) but many colourful people have lived or stayed here. On a September night in 1607 Sir Harry Ralt was a guest when a group of five strangers rode into town and created a scene outside an inn across the road. Enraged by their behaviour, Sir Harry leapt out of an upper window clutching his sword and dressed only in his nightshirt. He fought so well that the men were all put to flight, but the Mint House servants found him mortally wounded. His last words were unarguable: 'The knaves! I vow they durst not disturb my next sleep!' [23]

PIDDINGHOE

We'd like to put in a word for the people of Piddinghoe who, tradition says, shoe their magpies! This saying suggests the most extreme eccentricity — until you realise that, in days gone by, the black and white oxen were commonly known as magpies. [27]

PILTDOWN

Was Charles Dawson guilty or not guilty of the Piltdown Man hoax? (See *Piltdown* in *Hidden Sussex*, and *Ore* in this volume). The man who discovered a vein of natural gas at Heathfield, turned up a specimen of fish that was 'a cross between a goldfish and a carp', discovered a cart horse with an incipient horn and observed a 'sea serpent' in the English Channel on Good Friday, 1906, was given the nickname of 'the Sussex wizard'. But Dawson was, more soberly, a solicitor, clerk to Uckfield Urban District Council and to the Uckfield Magistrates and an elected member of several learned societies. Was he the hoaxer or the hoaxed? [12]

PLAISTOW

Plaistow Place is said (though it's much disputed) to have been the seat of Edward Lee, DD, who was Archbishop of York from 1531 until 1544. He took an active part in the Catholic uprising of 1536 which became known as the Pilgrimage of Grace. The house is also said to have been a summer residence for the archbishops of Canterbury at this time.   [2]

PLAYDEN

There was a leper hospital in Playden in 1379 and the man charged with running it, Robert de Burton, was accused of some disgraceful asset-stripping. He was said to have 'made waste, sale, destruction and dilapidation of the Hospital and its goods, to the final destruction of it'. Among the alleged offences was the felling of 75 large oaks for his own profit, and selling corn which should have been for the benefit of the poor. But what happened to him we don't know.

By an Act of 1678 a penalty of £5 was levied on the estates of people not buried in woollen cloth. But what happened if the family couldn't afford to comply? The Playden church records reveal that compassion could be shown. On December 4, 1700, Anne, the daughter of Robert and Elisabeth Walker, was buried. The record reads:

> 'Robert Walker haveing forfeited five pounds according to the Act of Parliament for burying in woollen, & the money paid in was disposed of to the sd. Robt. Walker being very poore by us
>
> — Thomas Rogeres, John Duke.'

[16]

PLUMPTON

Leonard Mascall, an early writer of books on various aspects of husbandry, lived at Plumpton Place. His first recorded work is a book of 1578 on planting and grafting trees and similar subjects, and there followed treatises on the rearing of cattle, poultry-breeding, fishing with hook and line and the trapping of vermin.

The scholar-shepherd John Dudeney was born in Plumpton on April 21, 1782. He became a shepherd when only eight years old and continued as such for 15 years — during which time he bought all the books he could afford. When he was 23, having educated himself widely in arithmetic, algebra, geometry, history and other subjects, he gave up his open-air life and became a schoolmaster in Lewes.   [21]

POLEGATE

Caleb Diplock thought he had left his considerable fortune to good causes. The trustees of his estate thought so, too. On his death they distributed the cash to a number of charities, including local hospitals, and they built a dozen flint cottages at Polegate as homes for poor people. But then relatives of the dead man arrived from Australia, contesting the will, and seven years later (in 1944) it was declared invalid by the Law Lords because of a technicality concerning its wording. The charities had to return all the money with interest, and the cottages were put on the market. Enter another wealthy man: the Black Cat cigarette millionaire Bernhard Baron. He gave the Quakers enough money to buy the cottages, and today they function very much as Caleb Diplock intended — as homes for elderly people in need. You'll see them a few hundred yards south of the junction of the A27 with the A22.   [**22/28**]

POLING

Sir Harry Johnston, a skilled naturalist, traveller and explorer who commanded the 1884 expedition to Kilimanjaro, bought the decayed priory here early in this century and commissioned his brother Philip to restore it. Sir Harry, who was a major influence in securing Nyasaland and Northern Rhodesia for Britain in the 1890s, later wrote a learned treatise on the Bantu languages, besides an autobiography and some fiction. He died in 1927. [**18**]

PORTSLADE

In 1795, the year in which the Prince of Wales rebuilt the Royal Pavilion at Brighton, his wife played the part of a holidaymaker at Copperas Gap, the old name for the coastal part of what was then a village. 'Last Monday,' runs a report from the time, 'the Princess of Wales took an airing to Copperas Gap, and there, attended by Lady Cholmondely, sat under a hedge upwards of two hours, where Her Royal Highness partook of refreshments, and being enlivened by the salubrity of the air, seemed to enjoy the rural scene with as much felicity as if she had been sitting under a canopy of state, and feasting on all the luxuries of the East!'   [**20**]

POSSINGWORTH

In the early 17th century the manor belonged to the Offley family, one of whom, Sir Thomas, had been Lord Mayor of London in 1566. It's recorded that he took his oath and went to Westminster with a pinnace 'deckyd with stremars and gonnes (guns) and dromes (drums).' He himself, however, was a man of frugal habits, inspiring the rhyme:

Offley three dishes had of daily rost,
An egg, an apple and (the third) a tost   [13]

POYNINGS

Sir Edward Poynings, then Lord Deputy of Ireland, in 1495 persuaded the Irish Parliament to pass a law making all the laws of England effective in Ireland and providing that no bill could be introduced into the Irish Parliament without prior sanction of the Council in England. This law was for many years known as Poynings' Law.

Up on the Devil's Dyke, in a caravan, lived the original Gipsy Lee. For over 30 years she told fortunes and was consulted by royalty and by scores of famous people, including Mr Gladstone, Lily Langtry, Adelina Patti and Mr Rothschild. Among her most remarkable predictions was that Edward VII's coronation would be postponed — as it was when he became ill. She died in 1911 in what was then known as Haywards Heath Mental Hospital.

[20]

PRESTON

The Rev James Douglas, formerly chaplain-in-ordinary to the Prince of Wales, accepted the curacy of Preston in 1810 and lived in the vicarage until his death nine years later. He'd been admitted to Holy Orders in 1780 after serving a period in the Austrian army, and he achieved fame for *Nenia Britannica*, a work published in stages from 1786 to 1793. This was 'A sepulchral History of Great Britain from the earliest period to its general conversion to Christianity; including a complete series of the British, Roman and Saxon sepulchral rites and ceremonies, with the contents of several hundred burial places, opened under a careful inspection of the author, tending to illustrate the early part of, and to fix on a more unquestionable criterion for, the study of antiquity.' His collection is in the Ashmolean Museum at Oxford.

An act of heroism in the first world war brought an end to the Stanford family line at Preston Manor. Vere Fane Benett-Stanford, the only male heir, in whom the highest hopes were placed, passed his own gasmask to one of his men during a German attack and subsequently died from the effects of poisoning.   [20]

PRINSTED

Under *Chidham* we mention the Case of the Three Vanished Chapels. One of these was at Prinsted, and the only reference we have found to it goes back to mid-Victorian times. It was then reported that 'no documents relative to this chapel have yet been found, but the building itself remains, for ages desecrated as a barn, and now used as a place of meeting by itinerant dissenters.' Well, the great John Wesley was once described in similar terms, so Prinsted chapel need not hang its head in shame.   [30]

PULBOROUGH

In March 1794 the young men of the village engaged with each other that they would learn the use of arms in case of a war. So they put themselves under the command of a drill sergeant of the Oxfordshire Militia. To Sussex, it seems therefore, belongs the honour of originating the volunteer movement which later became the Territorial Army — this Pulborough story is the earliest record known of a volunteer force.   [9/10]

PUNNETT'S TOWN

The great name among Sussex mill-owners is Dallaway; the family originally owned a mill here called Blackdown Mill, but it was burned down in 1859. So the then miller, Samuel Dallaway, bought from Biddenden in Kent Cherry Clack Mill, getting it transported here by Messrs. Hobden & Neve. It was set up in that same year, and Samuel worked it until his death in 1876. His sons Charles, Thomas and John all continued the family tradition both here and at Burwash. John's grandson Archie was still caring for it well into the 1970s. Archie decided in the aftermath of the 1939-45 war to restore his great-grandfather's mill to a working condition, and either bought replacement items from other mills or even made them himself. (See *Cowbeech, Stone Cross*).   [14]

PYECOMBE

Here is buried Nathaniel Payne Blaker, MRCS, a noted Sussex surgeon. Born in 1835, he became a student at Guy's Hospital in 1855, qualifying in 1858. In autumn 1859 he was appointed assistant surgeon in the Convict Hospital (as it then was) at Lewes. The next year saw him House Surgeon at the Brighton and Hove Dispensary in Queen's Road. He later became Surgeon at the Sussex County Hospital. He died in 1920, aged 85, by which time he had written a really fascinating book entitled *Sussex in Bygone Days*. It covers not only personal reminiscences but rural topics of all kinds.

In 1849 there came to light a most unpleasant murder. The victim, a local brewer named G.S. Griffith, was waylaid by highwaymen, robbed, shot and left for dead on the road near the Plough Inn. The murderers were never traced.   [20]

RACTON

The Gounter, or Gunter, family lived here for generations, their most famous representative being Colonel George, loyal supporter of Charles II (see *Bramber* and *Houghton*). In 1564 Arthur Gunter seems to have been the local godfather. This was soon after the passing of the Penal Acts which inaugurated the persecution of Catholics, among other things fining them heavily for failing to receive the Sacrament in their own churches at Easter. The Bishop of Chichester wrote a long report in which the people of Racton came in for some of the hardest knocks: 'These come not to their parish churches, nor receive the Holy Communion at Easter, but at that time get them out of the country until the feast be past....in the parish of Racton they have no churchwardens, clerk or collector for the poor, because of Mr Arthur Gunter, who rules the whole parish.'   [30]

RINGMER

Two American connections here. Gulielma Maria Postuma Springett married William Penn, the Quaker founder of Pennsylvania (see *Coneyhurst* in *Hidden Sussex*); and Anne Sadler married John Harvard, founder of the American University, in 1636 (see *South Malling*).

In *Hidden Sussex* we refer to the naturalist Gilbert White, who stayed at Delves House with his aunt Rebecca Snooke. (A later resident of the house was Sir Henry Wood, founder of the Promenade Concerts). Her husband was Henry Snooke, and we wonder if he can possibly be the man of that name who — according to the parish register of January 28, 1759 — was 'publicly reproved for his indecent behaviour and supercilious scoffs at the minister in sermon time'. Surely not!

Diagnosing insanity as opposed to eccentricity or downright perversity has always been a ticklish problem. The finger of suspicion points rather severely at a man named McDormand who had his wife incarcerated at Ringmer Lunatic Asylum in the 1850s. He claimed that he was unable to keep her at home because of her 'violent temper, inveterate intemperance and laxness in modesty'. But insanity? The visitors of the asylum thought not. They said she was kept without sufficient cause, and she was discharged. Louisa Hounsham was perhaps a more suitable case for treatment since it was entered in the records that she 'asserts and persists in maintaining that she is dead, in spite of all evidence to the contrary'.   [21]

RIPE

William Lulham was a humble yeoman who bettered himself, despite having joined Jack Cade's unsuccessful rising of 1450 (see *Cade Street*), and later bought the estate where he'd previously worked. He changed the name from Hallcourt to Lulhams but a later owner turned the clock back and it's now known as Hall Court Farm.

The novelist Malcolm Lowry, author of *Under the Volcano*, lived at White Cottage from 1956 until his death the following year.   [22]

RIVER

For Sir John Pelham, see introduction, page 11. [9]

ROBERTSBRIDGE

One of the curious medieval rituals was the bending of a silver penny over the head of anyone on whom a blessing was invoked. In the time of King Edward I pennies would regularly be bent over hawks at the end of the hawking season. About 1260 there lived in Robertsbridge Simon Croucher and his wife Catherine. She became ill during pregnancy, so the couple invoked the help of St. Richard de Wyche, bending a penny over her: she was delivered of a still-born child. Simon thereupon found another penny and again called to St. Richard for help, bending the coin over the child's body and signing its forehead with a cross. At once the child came to life, and opened its eyes. He was baptized, and four years later, well and happy, was produced as evidence in support of St. Richard's miracle.

The Cistercian Abbey founded by Alvred de St. Martin about 1176 became involved in a number of lawsuits, as the land was coveted by neighbours and the monks were at pains to defend it. Predatory booklovers, too, needed guarding against, and one of the Abbey books, now in the Bodleian, is inscribed, 'This book belongs to St. Mary of Robertsbridge; whosoever shall steal it or sell it, or in any way alienate it from this house, let him be anathema maranatha.' This spell did not prevent the book's coming into the possession of John, Bishop of Exeter, who excused himself by claiming that he did not know 'where the aforesaid house is.' We wonder whether he really tried very hard to find out.

The abbey offers a good needle-in-a-haystack story. In 1192 it was learnt that Richard Coeur-de-Lion, returning from Palestine, had been taken prisoner. The Abbots of Robertsbridge and Boxley were sent off to find him without so much as a clue. They travelled over a large part of the Low Countries and Germany, and eventually discovered him in Bavaria.

After the Dissolution in 1536, the abbey site was granted to Sir William Sidney. His successor, Sir Henry, was Lord Deputy of Ireland. Next came the great Sir Philip Sidney, soldier, scholar, wit and author of 'Arcadia', 'Astrophel and Stella', and other poems which have placed him securely in the front rank of Elizabethan lyricists (see *Lullington*). [14]

RODMELL

One of the strangest books on Sussex is *Nooks and Corners of Old Sussex*, by the Rev. P. de Putron, Rector of Rodmell from 1858 to 1891. It's worth having for its engravings, of exceptional interest. But even in 1875 the author had to complain that so many treasures of antiquity had been allowed to perish. What hope for us, writing after another 110 years of the onslaughts of man! [21]

ROEDEAN

The Founders of Roedean is a book we've recently been able to acquire. It was written by various members of the Lawrence family, who founded the famous school, and former pupils and staff. It tells in delightful manner the lives of a very human family circle. Penelope Lawrence, for instance, was a keen sportswoman, and was president at the inaugural dinner of the Women's Lacrosse Association. Eleven years later, she was again invited to preside. She unearthed a photograph of the first occasion and, looking at it, exclaimed, 'Heavens! I am going in the same dress I wore then! Do you think they will remember it?' But, whether 'they' did or no, that was the dress she wore.[20]

ROGATE

Even seven centuries ago official inquiries were corrupt and rigged, in somebody's eyes. In 1273, to be precise, Robert de Rogate wanted to build a mill beside Rogate bridge, where a ford existed across the river Rother. An inquiry certified that the construction of the mill would injure nobody, and Robert was authorized to proceed. However, Richard le Jay and Henry Husee disagreed, claiming that the mill, pool and sluices would obstruct the ford and make it impassable. They even apparently went so far as to obstruct the course of the building works. The story has a happy ending, though, because after negotiation the two protagonists, Robert and Henry, agreed that each would appoint a bridge warden to keep the ford clear and the bridge repaired, collecting a toll from bridge users and a maintenance contribution from other residents in the neighbourhood. **[29]**

ROTHERFIELD

For the last twelve years of her life Sophia Jex-Blake lived in the village. Born in 1840, she was the first woman to become qualified as a doctor, and she was a pioneer — militant at times — in the education of women. She died after a long and active life, in 1912. **[13]**

122

ROTTINGDEAN

The Rev. Thomas Hooker, the vicar here from 1792 to 1838, was lookout man for the local smugglers. The goods were landed below Saltdean and carried over the hill to the depots at Rottingdean along the line of what's now Whiteways Road. In her book *Smuggling in Kent and Sussex 1700-1840* Mary Waugh suggests that Rottingdean's exclusiveness has doubtful origins: 'Bearing in mind that this was a parish of shepherds and farmers, the fine old houses round the Green are indicative of an alternative source of wealth.'

Around 1880 a four-horse bus began to run from the Royal Oak. It carried a man with a posthorn, Charles Tupper, who was the champion posthorn player of England.

This area of coastline has always been a danger to shipping, and alongside smuggling activities the villagers have engaged in beach combing — often very profitably. It's recorded that many ships wrecked around the Isle of Wight had remains washed up the Channel to the Rottingdean promontory. One persistent beachcomber was "Scribbets" Holden whose sharp eyes never missed any unusual item among the pebbles. He's said to have found a gold ring lost eleven years earlier, and then found it for the second time after it was lost seven years later. But this is a fishing village, and ours may be another fisherman's tale.   [27]

ROWFANT

For years the house was the country seat of the Locker-Lampsons. Frederick Locker, who was born in 1821, started his working life in the Civil Service (he was clerk at Somerset House and then at the Admiralty) but he left about 1850 to devote himself to literature. In 1857 he published his first collection of poetry, *London Lyrics*, with an engraved frontispiece by no less a person than George Cruickshank. Ten years later there came an anthology called *Lyra elegantiarum* which immediately ran into trouble for including some poems by Walter Savage Landor which were copyright: the volume had to be reissued without them. In 1885 he took the double-barrelled surname by which he's known. A couple of his poems are included in the *Oxford Book of Victorian Verse*.   [5]

RUDGWICK

Sometimes one wonders why on earth a foreigner should choose to settle in a particular Sussex village. In the 13th century there lived here a man named Alard, who came from the Low Countries: he's referred to as Alard le Fleming. In 1260 he was clearly a man of substance, because Henry III granted him the right to hold a three-day fair around the Feast of Holy Trinity. In 1263 Alard died, possessed of his house, Newbridge, the advowson of the church and substantial lands. His estate was shared between his two daughters. One, Joan, was married to Henry Husee (see *Durford*); the other, Florence, was the wife of Walter de Lisle. In 1324 Newbridge (which no longer survives) was visited by Edward II.   [3]

RUNCTON

The abbey of Bruton in Somerset owned a chapel and lands here until the Dissolution, when the London grocer Thomas Bowyer bought the manor for the then large sum of £650. That was in 1540, and exactly a century later a descendant, also Thomas Bowyer, was created a baronet — probably for 'lending' a substantial sum to the hard-pressed Charles I.[25]

RUSHLAKE GREEN

An inscription from 1763 was recently found on a pane of glass at Pleydells:

> 'Abraham Holman is my name,
> and England is my nation;
> Rushlake was my Dwelling Place,
> but not long Habitation.'

It may be that Abraham was about to leave the village, but it's just as likely that he was referring to man's brief mortal span. [22]

RUSPER

Sir Isaac Shard of Rusper had such a reputation for meanness and greed that when the artist Hogarth was painting *The Miser's Feast* he could think of no better model for his central character. He had, however, reckoned without Sir Isaac's son, who presented himself at the great painter's studio, drew his sword and ripped a hole....in the canvas!

The firm of John Broadwood & Sons is the oldest manufactory of keyboard instruments in existence, and many members of the family are buried here. John Broadwood, a Scot, was born in 1732, was a cabinet-maker by trade and began making pianos in 1773. At first he made the old-fashioned 'square' pianos, but by 1781 at least he was making grand pianos approximating to the modern style. His sons joined him, and the company has continued to have Broadwoods among its directors until modern times. One of the most distinguished members of the family was Lucy Broadwood, an ardent collector of English folk music in the early part of the 20th century. She helped to found the English Folk Song Society, whose honorary secretary she was until 1908. [4]

RUSTINGTON

The Rustington Silver Band was brought into a property dispute back in 1908. The lord of West Preston manor, Thomas Bushby, erected sturdy gates at each end of Pigeon House Lane, claiming that the land within was his. Another land-owner, Tom Summers, insisted that the lane was a public right of way. The gates were pulled down and re-erected on several occasions until Summers enlisted the help of the band, which marched at the head of a procession playing martial music — and the gates were removed for the last time.

Sir Hubert Parry (1848-1918) lived here for much of his life. He was noted as a composer, his best-known work being *the* setting of Blake's *Jerusalem*, though he also did a magnificent choral version of Milton's *Blest Pair of Sirens*. He had become interested in music at an early age, composing hymn tunes when only eight, and achieved his degree of Bachelor of Music at Oxford *before* he actually entered the University. He became Professor of Music there in 1900, two years after receiving his knighthood. He died at Knight's Croft, Rustington, just a month before Armistice Day, 1918, and his ashes were placed in the crypt of St. Paul's Cathedral.

One can hardly fail to be moved by the story of the last sad years of the great dancer Vaslav Nijinsky. After years of being idolized by the ballet-lovers of half the world he suffered a collapse in 1918 while still only in his twenties. It was probably precipitated by a period of internment in Hungary during the first world war. Fortunately he had a devoted wife, Romola, who cared for him until his death after over 30 years of mental instability. The couple settled in England, where Nijinsky received the best treatment possible, and spent some years in a leased property in Surrey. The lease expired in 1949, but a complete stranger heard of their plight and offered them the use of his Rustington home. So Romola and Vaslav moved to the Sussex coast, and he enjoyed a few months of peace and good sea air before he died later in 1950.   **[26]**

RYE HARBOUR

Here we record the bravery of our lifeboat men and lament 17 needless deaths. At 4.50 on the morning of November 15, 1928, the coastguards were alerted that the Latvian steamer Alice was drifting in a terrible storm about three miles south west of Dungeness. The lifeboat, the Mary Stanford, was launched with great difficulty in the surging seas, and conditions were so bad that the men failed to spot the Verey lights which were fired to recall them only five minutes later — the steamer's crew had been rescued by another ship. At about 10.30 that morning, with weather conditions even worse, the Mary Stanford was overturned by a huge wave as she began to enter Rye Harbour, and every member of the crew perished. Rye Harbour is a separate community from Rye itself and in the 1920s was much smaller than it is today, so that there was scarcely a family in the little port village not touched by bereavement. There's a monument to the dead in the churchyard.   **[16]**

SADDLESCOMBE

When, early in the 14th century, the Knights Templars were suppressed for alleged blasphemy, sorcery and other crimes, their property at Saddlescombe was transferred to the rival military order of the Knights Hospitallers of St John of Jerusalem. The Hospitallers' most distinguished Grand Prior was Thomas Docwra (1501-1527) who attended Henry VIII at the Field of Cloth of Gold and came close to being elected the Order's Grand Master. In the event he remained more than 25 years as Prior of the Preceptory in this secluded Sussex valley. [20]

SAINT HILL

The house called Standen was built in the 1890s by the architect Philip Webb, a member of the William Morris movement which revolutionised late-Victorian attitudes to art and craftmanship: there are many Morris wallpapers and textiles here. Webb was a painstaking and strongminded man who concerned himself with every aspect of design and had no time for the whims of the people who paid his fees. On the completion of Standen the owner gave him a silver snuffbox bearing an inscription to the effect that when a client talked nonsense Webb resorted to a pinch of snuff! [5]

SALEHURST

Sir Alan Boxhull, of Salehurst in 1378 perpetrated one of the most shocking violations of sanctuary ever recorded. With a party of 50 armed men he burst into Westminster Abbey during High Mass in pursuit of two fugitive knights. One of them, Robert Hawley, was chased twice round the quire before falling dead with a dozen sword wounds in front of the Prior's stall. For four months afterwards the Abbey was closed to all religious rites, and even sittings of Parliament were suspended for fear of contamination through assembling so near the scene of the outrage. [14/15]

SALTDEAN

The Duke of Cumberland, a local resident at the end of the 18th century, was one of the originators of yacht racing in England. [27]

SAYERS COMMON

The reminiscences in old age of James Nye, born in the village in 1835, included the days when Stroods was a coaching stage-post with up to 100 horses stabled there. He recalled that when the railway was being built as many as 16 horses would pull one huge waggon loaded with equipment for the making of Clayton tunnel. 'My father had me over at Hassocks to peep through the palings to see one of the first trains go by. The carriages were only open waggons.' [20]

SCAYNES HILL

The Rev. Frederic Willett came to live in mid-Sussex in 1881 and for 25 years had entire charge of St Augustine's church without receiving a penny for it — Scaynes Hill wasn't made a separate ecclesiastical district until 1930. He tried running the nearby Anchor Inn as 'a model public house', but for several entirely foreseeable reasons it never worked. On June 16, 1938, he celebrated his 100th birthday, having preached his last sermon only six years earlier.   [12]

SEDGWICK

John de Maunsel was evidently a good churchman (he was several times offered bishoprics and refused) and something of a wastrel (he died abroad in dire poverty and wretchedness around 1263). He held the manor of Sedgwick, which passed to Simon de Montfort the younger after John's death and was then the subject of a lawsuit for ownership following the Battle of Evesham. The court favoured John le Savage's claim over that of William de Braose, perhaps because John was already in possession. The later history of Sedgwick takes us through many of the most eminent Sussex families — de Say, Greville, Mowbray, Howard, Caryll and the Dukes of Richmond among them.   [3]

SEDLESCOMBE

Early one morning in December 1764 the sifting house of Sedlescombe powdermills blew up with a ton of gunpowder inside. Among the four men killed were James and Thomas Gilmore, the only sons of the proprietor.   [24]

SELHAM

Not far from here was a bridge over the River Rother beside which grew, in the early 19th century, a large and overhanging willow. The local excise officer was a Welshman named Warren who was an ardent, even ruthless, upholder of the law. One night a party of smugglers while about their business happened to meet Warren by this tree. They captured him and suspended him by his hair with a cord tied round a branch so that his body was dangling in the river and his head only just clear of the water. He remained like this for a good while until his cries for help attracted some passers-by (a lucky fluke, since the area was sparsely populated) who untied him and fished him out of the water. Warren, who was none the worse for his adventure, later left the excise service and became a farmer.   [9]

SELMESTON

Rev. William Douglas Parish, born 1833, came as vicar to Selmeston in 1863. He has two claims to local fame: first, he edited the Sussex Domesday Book for the Sussex Archaeological Society, and second, he compiled *A Dictionary of the Sussex Dialect*, published in 1875, recently enlarged and reissued, but never supplanted. It is not merely a word list, but includes a sizeable section on Sussex sayings and crafts. To whet your appetite for this utterly compelling book, we recount the reply of a lady asked for her opinion of a lately-deceased relative: 'But there, I'll give 'er 'er doo, she 'ad 'er good faults as well as 'er bad ones.' [22]

SELSEY

St. Wilfrid must have been a remarkable man for any age: we recount a bit of his story under *Church Norton*, as well as in *Hidden Sussex*. He was the first of the bishops of the old see of Selsey. The twenty-fourth and last was Stigand, consecrated in 1070. He was the first Norman bishop, and as it was a strong part of Norman policy to have bishops in larger towns, he abandoned Selsey for Chichester after a mere five years. He moved out the nuns of St. Peter's church and immediately started on the building of a new cathedral. However, he died in 1087 and when a successor, Luffa, was elevated four years later, he pulled down most of Stigand's work and started again. [25]

SELSFIELD

Public conscience used to be rather different from what it is today. A person making his will might leave his money for the public good in a way which would astonish us. For instance, Richard Culpeper, of the *Ardingly* family, left a tidy sum of money for repairing the road from Wakehurst to 'Seldwyke Cross', the old name of Selsfield. Still, his descendants may well have been the principal users of the road at that time. [4]

SHARPTHORNE

During World War II, when Holland was overrun by the Nazis, the Dutch Royal Family escaped to Britain, and spent most of the War period in this country. The young Princess Beatrix spent some time in a house here, enjoying at least comparative peace. [5]

SHEFFIELD PARK

Lord Sheffield has several claims on our attention, but we liked a minor story. In 1765 he imported from Ireland a rarity — potatoes — for his newly-acquired Sheffield estate. Nobody knew what to do with them, until at last a road worker from a distant county was found who would plant them regularly on Old Lady Day. There was a strong prejudice against the vegetable (the usual dinner accompaniment had always been pease pudding), and at the elections at Lewes at the period, it shared with Popery the indignation of the populace. The great election slogan was, 'No Popery — no potatoes!'

Lord Sheffield's daughter was Maria Josepha Holroyd, who married Lord Stanley of Alderley. Her letters written between 1776 and 1796, when she was the lady of Sheffield Park, have been published. She was much interested in the fine gardens, laid out by Humphrey Repton, one of the greatest landscape gardeners. [12]

SHERMANBURY

Dr. John Bear, Rector of Shermanbury for over fifty years in the 18th century, married a widow whose son from her first marriage was Dr. John Burton, a sundry learned scholar in Greek and Latin. When Burton visited his mother in 1751 he was repelled by the coarseness of the Sussex folk he met. He commented in his journal (which fortunately he wrote in either Greek or Latin at choice) on 'the awkward prodigality and sordid luxury of their feasts; the inelegant roughness and dull hilarity of their conversation; their intercourse with servants and animals so assiduous, with clergymen or gentlemen so rare; being illiterate, they shun the lettered; being sots, the sober....' [10/11]

SHIPLEY

In the church is a large alabaster tomb to Sir Thomas Caryll (died 1616), his wife Margaret and their family. There is a long inscription, including eight lines of pompous verse. Judging by the vast quantities of such inscriptions, writing epitaph verse in the 17th and 18th centuries must have been like writing birthday cards today — the wonder is how such an infinite supply can possibly be maintained.

Thomas Paine, author of 'The Rights of Man', was born in Norfolk in 1737, but lived in Lewes for some six years. His extreme radical views made him unpopular, but he did have his supporters. One such, parish clerk at Shipley, made several public speeches in support of Paine, and was so hated for it that in 1793 he was burned in effigy before his own front door during a demonstration uncommonly rowdy even for those forthright times. [10]

SHULBREDE

The priory was founded by Ralph de Arden in about 1200. Building proceeded smoothly, and by 1242 Prior John was able to arrange to take scholars, rather like a medieval boarding school. His successor, however, seems to have been rather less enthusiastic. About 1249 an upper-class yeoman, John de Aguillon, came to a deathbed arrangement with the prior that for a sum of over £5 his executors should place his son Godfrey in the priory for seven years, to be trained for holy orders, and that Godfrey should then either be received as a canon or have his money returned. The rest can almost be guessed: in 1263 Godfrey had to make a formal complaint to the Assize Court that he had neither been received as a canon nor got his money back. Another case to refer to a medieval trading standards office...? [1]

SIDLESHAM

A Chichester merchant with the wonderful name of Woodroffe Drinkwater built the only tide mills in West Sussex here. According to Dallaway a full load of wheat could be ground in an hour.

Sidlesham's was probably the last village band in Sussex to play regularly in church. It flourished until the mid-1840s and accompanied a group of singers at most services. The end came when the then vicar, the Rev. Goddard, proposed the introduction of simple psalm-singing, whereupon all the performers — singers and instrumentalists alike — gathered up their instruments and music books and stalked out of the church in high dudgeon. It's not recorded whether the good minister ever retracted his views. [25]

SIDLEY

We don't have ratcatchers any more — only rodent operatives. But 'Old John' of Sidley Green wasn't too proud to admit his calling. During the 1840s there was a board outside his cottage which read:

> *Old John, rats a catcher, of when I am able,*
> *In pantry, outhouse, barn and stable,*
> *With ferrets fierce and dogs so sure;*
> *My donkey's lean and I am poor* [24]

SINGLETON

In the days of Queen Victoria, when Goodwood Races were the climax of the Summer Season, Singleton was the home of many racegoers, as the stables were of many fine horses. The Prince of Wales (later Edward VII) kept his racehorses here and was a regular visitor. [17]

SLAUGHAM

The Covert family, centred here, were great Sussex landowners. Tradition has it that they could travel from London to the sea without leaving their own manorial land. In William Covert's 1494 will he left 6s. 8d. to every poor priest or clerk within five miles of Slaugham who wished to go to a University, and a similar sum to every poor maiden lacking a friend, towards her marriage. Sir Walter Covert in 1600 built Slaugham Place, but the family

fell upon evil days and soon died out. By 1785 the house was in ruins, still visible by the public footpath from the churchyard. They're on private property, but the owners tell us that they are working to restore them so that they can be opened.

In more recent times Slaugham was the home of the romantic novelist Denise Robins. [4]

SLINDON

Stephen Langton (born about 1150) was consecrated archbishop of Canterbury in 1207, in Viterbo. King John refused to confirm his appointment, so he remained abroad for six years. At last he came to England, becoming one of the most influential draftsmen of Magna Carta (1215). In 1228 Langton, still archbishop, breathed his last in the former palace of the archbishops whose site is now occupied by Slindon House. A tablet to Langton's memory was placed in Slindon church in 1930 by Miss Rhoda M.M. Langton, a direct descendant. [18]

SLINFOLD

In 1517 the manor of Drungewick came into the possession of Sir Henry Hussey (also spelt Hussee), a distinguished Roman Catholic — not as easy to be then as now. He had sufficient standing to be chosen in 1555 by Queen Mary Tudor to be a member of a deputation to go to Rome 'to confirm the reconciliation of the nation with the Catholic church' — alas, short lived. The manor was transferred by the Husseys to the Duke of Norfolk about 1660.

A later Slinfoldian was the rector James Dallaway, author of the first section of the earliest history of West Sussex. He was presented to the sinecure rectory of Slinfold in 1803, but continued to hold the living of Leatherhead in Surrey, where he lived until his death in 1834. [18]

131

SMALL DOLE

Woods Mill, north of the village, is now the headquarters of the Sussex Trust for Nature Conservation, thanks to a generous gift from the family of Dr J.N. Douglas-Smith in 1966. The ownership of the mill can be clearly traced from at least 1647, although there seems to have been a mill here back as far as Domesday. In 1883 it was rented by Charles Coote, who later purchased the freehold and ran the business until his death in 1916. His son Caleb took it on until 1927. He was the last miller, because it was soon afterwards converted into a tea-garden.   [20]

SOCKNERSH

Those extravagant singers Tom Jones and Engelbert Humperdinck bought Socknersh Manor near Burwash in the seventies but never lived there. We'd like to mention two men who did — the brothers Increased and Changed Collins. These are further examples of 17th century Puritan names, and the real wonder is that their older brother was named simply Thomas! Increased, not content with his name, later took the title Captain of Motes and Bulwark in Dover.   [14]

SOMPTING

William Brownsword, an 18th century vicar here, must have been something of a wag. Among his publications were 'a poem serio-comic' entitled 'Laugh and lye down; or, a pleasant but sure remedy for the gout, without expense or danger' and 'Laugh upon Laugh, a poem aethico-comico-satyrical, by the Rev. W. Brownsword, Vicar of Sompting, 1740'. He was vicar from 1707 to 1749, so he can't have been bad at his job. But what was his true name? We've given it as spelt in Lower's *Worthies of Sussex*, and a rather romantic name it is, but the Sompting church guide gives the more prosaic 'Broadwood'.
                                                                               [19]

SOUTHBOURNE

West of the village, straddling the A27, is an area called Hermitage which in pre-reformation days was the site of a hermit's hovel. Hermits were frequently stationed near city gates or other strategic points, and this one was especially required to collect donations towards the upkeep of the bridge here. The bishop would grant hermits a privilege entitling them to sell indulgences for a small sum of money to passing travellers. No doubt this dated from times when most travellers would have been pilgrims, but by Tudor times a hermit was no more than what the Law calls 'a sturdy beggar'.

A local resident whose name will be familiar to boating enthusiasts is Alan J. Watts, author of a number of authoritative books on yachting and kindred pursuits — *Wind and Sailing Boats, Instant Weather Forecasting* and *Weather Forecasting Ashore and Afloat*, to name a few.   [30]

SOUTHEASE

During the 17th century Southease manor held land across the river at Heighton, and tenants there had to send labourers over to reap the manor corn for a set number of days each year. The reapers were required to be at Stockferry by sunrise. When the weather was unsuitable the farmer had to be at the ferry in time to send them away: if he was late and the reapers had already crossed over, it was reckoned a day's work. With money going to waste in wages for no work done we don't suppose the farmer was often late — even in those days before the invention of alarm clocks! [21]

SOUTHERHAM

Another anonymous story. This small village was at one time a chapelry of South Malling but ceased to be so in the early 1800s. When the chapel itself came to be demolished in the 1830s the skeleton of a man was found embedded in the north wall. There was no record of any interment and it's now thought most likely that he was the founder of the chapel. [21]

SOUTH MALLING

There used to be a palace of the Archbishops of Canterbury here, and to this place came the four knights who had just murdered Thomas à Becket. 'On entering the house, they threw off their arms and trappings on the large dining-table which stood in the hall, and after supper gathered round the blazing hearth; suddenly the table started back, and threw its burden on the ground. The attendants, roused by the crash, rushed in with lights and replaced the arms. But soon a second crash was heard, and the various articles were thrown still farther. One of the conscience-stricken knights suggested it was indignantly refusing to bear the sacrilegious burden of their arms'. (From Dean Stanley).

Famous names associated with South Malling include the 17th century diarist John Evelyn who, as a boy, laid one of the first stones when the church was built (his grandfather largely financed it) and John Harvard, whose will provided for the building of Harvard College in America. It was here on April 19, 1636, that he married Anne Sadler, daughter of the vicar of Ringmer. Why wasn't she married in her own church? Harvard was a Puritan and almost certainly chose the nearby parish to avoid compromising his father-in-law. [21]

SOUTHOVER

The first prior of Lewes was Lanzo, who ruled the foundation from 1077 to 1107. The first building work was of the church, consecrated in 1098. This would have included the sanctuary area around the high altar, and Lanzo lived to see the interment of Lady Gundrada in 1085 and her husband Earl William de Warenne (see *Introduction*), who died in 1088.

In 1512 Agnes Morley founded the Free Grammar School in her will. She made a separate document, called her testament, in which she went into all the necessary detail. 'A messuage and garden next to the mylle called Watergate... shall serve for a scolemaister and an usher there to dwell in, to tech grammar in the same forever... I will that my ...cheste shall stand in the parrishe churche of Southovere aforesaide, which cheste shalhave iij diverse keys .. the Prior of Lewes shalhave oone keye, the churchwardeynes of Southover ... shalhave an other key, and Thomas Puggislee thelder and his heires shalhave an other keye ...' She took care, did Agnes.   [21]

SOUTHWATER

Even such a seemingly modern community as this owes something to a departed benefactor. In this case it's the church, built about 1850. Sir Henry Fletcher, Bart., gave the land for the church and yard, and contributed handsomely to the construction cost. And Sir Henry is not forgotten — there's a window to him, prominently placed.   [10]

SOUTHWICK

Here in 1611 was born John Pell, a mathematical prodigy. By the time he graduated for his B.A., aged only 17, he was not only a complete master of figures, but spoke and wrote in eight languages. He lived much of his life at Steyning, but in 1643 became Professor of Mathematics at Amsterdam University. Anthony à Wood described him as a helpless man whose relations kept him in want of necessaries, even ink and paper, to his dying day. But he wrote a number of treatises, and is credited with the invention of the division sign $\div$ which we still use today.   [20]

STANMER

If you think that ploughing with oxen as pulling power went out with the Middle Ages, you're wrong. Teams of black oxen were in use in various parts of East Sussex till late in the last century, while at Stanmer the Earl of Chichester, whose family built Stanmer Place in the early 18th century, kept his ox teams until well on into the present one.   [21]

STANSTED

Stansted goes back to Norman days, and old chronicles show that Henry II was here on several occasions. But it's now owned by the Earl of Bessborough, whose family moved here from Ireland after their stately home was burnt down in 1920: they looked throughout England for somewhere to house the pictures, furniture and other treasures which had been saved. The tenth earl wrote a book about Stansted, published in 1958 as *A Place in the Forest*: a successor, *Enchanted Forest*, appeared in 1984.[**30**]

STAPLE CROSS

Young William Goodsell was convicted of setting fire to a barn here in November 1833, presumably during the disturbances known as the Swing Riots. When he was hanged at Horsham gaol over a thousand people, including many women and children, watched the grisly performance.[**15**]

STAPLEFIELD

Blessed as it is with a beautiful village green, Staplefield has long been the centre of social and sporting associations. In 1919, a few months after the end of the first world war, Mrs Ludwig Messel decided to organize May Day revels, and they were for years a regular annual event under her guidance. Her husband, Lt. Col. Messel, was owner of Nymans at Handcross and one of the chief architects of its wonderful gardens. The famous theatrical designer and artist Oliver Messel was their son.   [**4**]

STEDHAM

The present church is 19th century, but there was a previous one on the same site, where in the 14th century one Simon was rector. In the early years of the 19th century a seal matrix was dug up on Cissbury Hill. It bore a picture of St Michael slaying the dragon, with an ecclesiastic praying to him. The wording round the edge was in Latin and said 'The seal of Simon, rector of the church of Stedham'. As Stedham is a full 20 road miles from Cissbury, we wonder what Simon could have been doing, so far from home and carrying his official seal with him.

Sir Charles Taylor (1770-1857) was a 'character' whose end was appropriately contentious. He detested lawyers and always ended family prayers with the words: 'From all attorneys and lawyers, and from their devilish machinations, Good Lord deliver us.' Having become very deaf, he resented not being able to take part in dinner-table conversations and would interrupt them by the furious ringing of a handbell. And his end? The story is that when he died the horses refused to draw the hearse with his coffin in it. Instead they pulled an empty hearse while six men had to carry the coffin eight miles to Stedham Church.[8]

STEYNING

William Cowerson, who's buried in Steyning churchyard, was killed during the last major smuggling battle in West Sussex. He was one of a group of men wielding bats and staves to protect the smugglers. Contraband was landed on Worthing beach on a bright moonlit night in February 1832. Cowerson, a Steyning stonemason who had been repairing West Tarring church in daylight hours, broke a customs officer's arm with his bat. The officer, a Lt Henderson, had a gun in his other hand and shot Cowerson dead.

The affair between Charles Stewart Parnell and Kitty O'Shea ruined his political career in Ireland and the pair spent the latter part of their lives in Sussex. They were married at Steyning register office on June 25, 1891. Parnell was to die months afterwards in Hove, but Kitty lived on until 1921, dying at Littlehampton.   [19]

STOKE, North and South

Laurence Elliot was the water bailiff in charge of the South Stoke swannery in 1713 and he compiled a full list of the duties of fishermen, beadles and under-bailiffs of the River Arun. He included a list of the various swan-marks and noted that 'the fine paid by the heir, upon coming to the estate, to the water-bailiff was 6s and 8d for every renewal of the swan mark'. Swans were a great delicacy in those days, and part of his job was to watch out for poachers.

A headstone in North Stoke churchyard is dedicated to the memory of Martha (died September 12, 1766) and Robert (died June 2, 1774) Newell. It carries a couplet: 'We hope there change is for the best/To live with Christ and be at rest.' The use of the words 'we hope' doesn't make it sound as if the writer of the couplet was very confident about it.   [18]

STONE CROSS

The mill was built in the 19th century for Samuel Dallaway, cousin and name-sake of the original owner at *Punnett's Town*. His grandson, who ran the business until 1937, was the last of that great milling family to work a mill commercially. [**28**]

STONEGATE

Andrew Young was a Presbyterian minister who became an Anglican, and he was rector here from 1941-1959. He published his *Collected Poems* while at Stonegate and later, after he retired to Yapton, brought out other books such as *The Poet and the Landscape*. [**14**]

STOPHAM

The Barttelot (or Bartlett) family were lords of the manor of Stopham for generations, and the church holds many family monuments. John Barttelot (died 1428) was Treasurer to the Household of the Earl of Arundel; so was his son, also John, who died 1453. Later in the 15th century came Richard, who died in 1482 and is buried here with his wife Petronilla. In 1601 William died, and another Richard (died 1614) is also buried here with his two wives. There are brasses to them all in the church, all in good condition or better, and fascinating to students of costume. But please don't rub them; each rubbing destroys a bit of the surface and before long there will be nothing left for future generations to enjoy. [**9**]

STORRINGTON

Storrington has given a home to several important people, but the best-known is probably Francis Thompson. He was a poet who lived from 1859 to 1907, and was befriended by the Meynells, Wilfrid and Alice, also poets (see *Greatham*). Thompson's life was dogged by poverty and ill-health, yet he found much comfort from membership of the Roman Catholic Church. He is now best remembered for the magnificent 'The Hound of Heaven', and a charmingly sentimental shorter piece, 'Ex ore infantium.' Much of his best work dates from his time in Sussex.

Here, too, lived an eminent soldier, Sir Hollis Bradford, KCB. He fought at Copenhagen, Corunna, Flushing, Salamanca, Vittoria and lastly at Waterloo, when he received a wound from which he died eighteen months later. [**19**]

STOUGHTON

When St. Wilfrid (see *Church Norton* and *Hidden Sussex*) came to our county he took refuge with Aethelwalh, king of the South Saxons, who was already a Christian, though his people were not. Wilfrid converted them and established the church in Sussex. Some years later he was sought out by one Caedwalla, whom Eddius Stephanus called 'an exile of noble birth' but John Godfrey 'a daring young adventurer'. Caedwalla's marauders met Aethelwalh's forces on Bow Hill over-looking Stoughton village. Aethelwalh was slain, and Wilfrid prudently transferred his allegiance to Caedwalla, who gave him a quarter of the Isle of Wight in return. [**17**]

STREAT

Robert Chatfield came of a long-established Ditchling family, but he lived much of his life at nearby Streat. His main claim to fame is that he founded the Old Meeting House at Ditchling, for in his 1735 will he refers to 'a house built belonging to me for the Baptist to Meeting' (?meet in) 'and land to bury their Dead in at Ditchling Town . . .' He died in January 1736, and was the third person to be buried in the land he gave.   [21]

STRETHAM

Robert Sherburn was bishop of Chichester from 1508 to 1536, and held a manor here. His steward was one Thomas Stapylton, who may have been the father of the distinguished Thomas Stapleton, born at Henfield and one of the great 16th century theologians.   [20]

SULLINGTON

The Rev. George Palmer was rector of the old Saxon/Norman church from 1824 until his death in 1858, being succeeded by his son Henry who held the post until 1927 — so that for a period of more than a century Sullington had only two rectors, and those were father and son! Henry kept a workaday

diary for 65 years, in which he interspersed factual notes with lively comment. Thus, 'Drove with A....to West Wantley, where Mrs X. was found wholesomely dirty...' Or, 'En route to Stopham the foolish horse as nearly turned us over as anything; my mother behaved fairly well...' Or, 'Changed my sermon tactics.'   [19]

SUTTON

John Sargent was Visitor, or overseer, of the large 'house of industry' for paupers in the 18th century. The paupers were let out for work, generally on a contract basis, in exchange for food and clothing — and doubtless had to work hard for meagre reward. An announcement in the 1790s wooed contractors with "the benefit of the paupers' labour, and the occupation of a convenient and well-furnished house and building, with a garden and two meadows...A manufactory, either for spinning coarse wools, or for making worsted, may be easily established on the premises, as both these have been lately carried on there, and the utensils for boath are nearly complete."   [9]

TANGMERE

Many brave men served at the Tangmere aerodrome between 1917 and 1958: pilots based here played a vital role in the Battle of Britain in 1940. There have been men known for other reasons, too: the novelist H.E. Bates (*The Go Between* and the books featuring the Larkin family) served here, as did Group Captain Peter Townsend who nearly married Princess Margaret. But we'd like to highlight the rather eccentric behaviour of Squadron Leader C.N. Lowe, a former English rugby international and wartime pilot, who in 1930 'having read that two American airmen had flown their machines tied together decided that his whole squadron would improve on that'. The military aviation museum's booklet, from which we quote, informs us that No. 43 Squadron duly demonstrated the very first tied-together formation aerobatics with twelve aircraft! [17]

TARRING NEVILLE

We mention the Rev. Diones Geere under *Denton*. Two reverend men of the same name, father and son, were ministers both at Denton and here. The father was rector from 1738 until 1765, the son's dates being 1774 to 1831. Cliff Cottage was the home of the novelist Angela Thirkell during 1936.[21]

TARRING West

Another of St Richard's miracles. While he was forced out of his See (the story's told under *Ferring*) he lived for some time at West Tarring with the rector, Simon. After cattle had badly damaged a tree in Simon's garden Richard cut a graft from another and, though it was late July and quite the wrong time of year, 'the graft grew and bore flowers and fruit that same year'. [19]

TELHAM

There's a charming story about the name of this little hamlet between Battle and Hastings. An old tradition says that the place existed in the time of William the Conqueror and that just before the Battle of Hastings his army was lined up for him, on horseback, to 'tell 'em over'. Augustus Hare, the Victorian writer whose book on Sussex is dated 1896, recounts the old story as if it were fact (though he pounces severely on the inaccuracies of other writers). Alas, a more scientific study of place names gives him the lie. It was spelt as it is now as long ago as the Assize Rolls of 1288 and in the Battle Abbey Custumal of about the same period. R.G. Roberts found that Tella was the name of a monk and the 'ham' part meant either a home or an enclosure. So it was Tella, not the Conqueror, who left his name for posterity. [24]

TELSCOMBE

Ambrose Gorham ran a string of racehorses which were trained on the gallops on Telscombe Tye. In 1902 his horse, Shannon Lass, won the Grand National and Gorham celebrated by restoring the church. A considerable landowner, he later had the so-called Village Club built for the locals. He gave the children each a book and a pair of wellington boots every Christmas, and he arranged for them to learn dancing. He died in 1933, and 'Gorham's Gift' established a charitable trust, one of its obligations being the distribution of money to poor women on St Thomas' Day (December 21), traditionally known as Gooding Day in Sussex. So that the village should remain unspoilt (compare the totally separate Telscombe Cliffs) he bequeathed his large estate to Brighton Corporation.   [21/27]

TERWICK

Another benefactor. After her husband died in the 1850s Lady Dorothy Nevill made the gardens of Dangstein House famous. In 1861 she built an aviary and a school for the village. The long and charming garden avenue she created was always afterwards known as Lady Dorothy's Walk. [29]

THAKEHAM

Stephen Shortred clearly had no time for the clergy. The parish registers of the 1620s show that the authorities several times complained about him to the bishop or archdeacon, on one typical occasion 'for reproaching defaming and reviling our minister in rude and unreverend speeches, saying he is a hippocrite and a devill. And he said he is a spitefull priest and bad and the turd in his teeth.'

We learn, too, that Elizabeth Feild was 'delivered of a baseborne childe in the howse of Edward Duke; the reputed father is William Parson, as the common fame goeth'.   [10]

THORNEY, West

Edward the Confessor's chaplain in the early 11th century was one Thomas Osberne. On his being appointed Bishop of Exeter the king gave him the lands and churches of Appledram, Bosham, Chidham, Funtington and Thorney — which is why the Bishop of Exeter's permission often had to be obtained for anything new in the south west corner of Sussex. The gift was intended to yield an income for the Devon See, and one of the payments which the people of Thorney had to make to the bishop was 700 oysters on the Sunday of mid-Lent every year. That doesn't seem much like Lenten abstemiousness to us!   [30]

TICEHURST

John Wybarne died in 1490, having been twice married. His second wife Agnes, who died in 1503, wished to be buried in her husband's grave in the chancel of Ticehurst church, and directed her executors 'to bye a convenient stone to laye upon my husband John Wybarne's grave and myne'. What her executors did was to take over an earlier brass (perhaps of about 1350), add a new inscription to the old figure and depict his two wives, half height, one on either side of a figure supposed to be John Wybarne but in fact wildly anachronistic, being actually dressed in a style of a hundred years earlier![14]

TIDE MILLS

William Catt, who ran the mill and its ancillary industrial concerns near Bishopstone in the mid 19th century, visited France on several occasions to advise King Louis Philippe on how to construct tide mills. When revolution drove the monarch into exile he and his queen sailed for England, landed at Newhaven and were met by Catt. He must have had a sound knowledge of local practice since, staying overnight at the Bridge Hotel, he signed the register in the names of 'Mr and Mrs Smith'! [27]

TILLINGTON

Despite our story under *Ashburnham*, the tradition exists that on the scaffold Charles I gave his watch to Sir Thomas Herbert of Tillington. Perhaps the king had two watches. On the other hand, perhaps not: research in the early histories of the county has failed to bring to light any such person. No such uncertainty surrounds John Keyse Sherwin, born in these parts in 1753. He was a woodcutter on the Petworth estate until one day he saw some of the Mitford family at Pitshill doing some drawings. He was fascinated and was allowed to try, being given a pencil which his rough hands could hardly hold. His first effort, however, was so good that it was presented to the Society of Arts, who promptly awarded him their silver medal! He was sent to London for proper tuition and within three years achieved the Society's prize medal. He was later appointed engraver to George III and was awarded the Royal Academy's gold medal. But the pressures of London life proved too much for him: he began to live in a manner discreetly called 'irregular' and died in poverty in 1790 at the age of 37.

One of the county's most distinguished divines, Bishop Samuel Wilberforce, planted a group of trees here which has always been known as Bishop's Clump. [9]

TORTINGTON

Lady Hadvinia Corbet founded a small priory here, probably in the 12th century, and dedicated it to St Mary Magdalen. It housed five or six Augustinian canons. Some architectural remains are still visible. [18]

TREYFORD

In *Hidden Sussex* we tell the story of the Victorian church which was built here as the 'Cathedral of the Downs'. The cost of its building — it was consecrated in 1849 — was met by the wealthy patroness of the living, the Hon. Mrs. Vernon Harcourt, who then owned the entire parish of 1,260 acres. She was the sister of Henry John Peachey, the third Lord Selsey. He died childless in 1838 so his sister took the whole estate — and there were no death duties to pay! It had been bought in the 1770s by, we think, his grandfather, who even in those days had paid £13,200 for it.   [8]

TROTTON

Thomas Otway (1652-1685) is one of the less happy notables recorded in this book. He was a poet and dramatist still remembered for 'Venice Preserv'd', 'The Soldier's Fortune' and other plays — he was once thought comparable with Shakespeare. His father, Rev. Humphry Otway, was curate of Trotton, and in very humble circumstances. Upon Humphry's death, Thomas, then aged 19, went to London, became an actor with little success, and started writing plays instead. His fourth play, 'Friendship in Fashion', was revived in 1749 but hissed off the Drury Lane stage for immorality and obscenity. 'Venice' was his last work, produced shortly before his death; for its copyright he received a mere £15, insufficient to keep him in health. He died, it has been claimed, of alternate starvation and excess, before reaching the age of 34. He is best recalled in Samuel Johnson's *Lives of the English Poets*.   [8]

TURNER'S HILL

The story of Jacob Harris (see *Wivelsfield* in *Hidden Sussex*) was one of the more lurid bits of Sussex history. It was actually at Turner's Hill that Harris was apprehended.

The hamlet is an old one, and grew up at the junction of two medieval roads whose line is closely followed today. But we're sorry to say that the first Turner wasn't a highwayman. The name goes back to the family of Galfridus le Turnur as long ago as 1296. None of the old Sussex historians mentions them so probably they were just local farmers.   [5]

TWINEHAM

Richard Stapley in his diary tells of a monster trout.

"In ye month of November, 1692, there was a trout found in ye Poyningswish, in Twineham, which was 29 inches long from ye top of ye nose to ye tip of ye taile; and John fflint had him and eat him. He was left in a low slank after a ffloode, and ye water fell away from him, and he died. The fish I saw at John fflint's house ye Sunday after they had him; and at night they boiled him for supper, but could not eat one halfe of him; and there was six of them at supper; John fflint and his wife Jane, and four of their children; and ye next day they all fell on him again and compassed him."   [11]

UCKFIELD

Fanny Burney passed through in 1779 with Mrs Thrale and declared that she found nothing to interest her but an epitaph which read: 'A wife and 8 little children had I/And two at birth who never did cry'.

Edward Daniel Clarke, who was born here, was a fellow of Jesus College, Cambridge who in 1801 accepted the curacy of his native village — until, somehow, his name got put down for the 'Supplementary Militia'. Then, in dread of having to enter the army, he disqualified himself by taking up a college appointment. 'Tell the Master,' he wrote to a friend, 'that I will be bursar, shoeblack, or even gip, sooner than march in the awkward squad with a mob of undrilled recruits, with the certainty of being brought to a court-martial for disobedience of orders.' Still, his return to academic life secured his fame, because in 1802/3 he toured Norway and Sweden in the company of Mr (later Professor) Malthus and the future Bishop Otter of Chichester, who wrote Clarke's biography. [12]

UDIMORE

'Village Shopkeeper Captures German Pilot' was the headline in the Sussex Express when a special constable, Eric Field, earned a little glory for himself during the second world war. A Messerschmitt had been shot down, and Mr Field locked the pilot up in his shop until the Army arrived. He became the proud possessor of an official 'receipt' for his prisoner![24]

UPPER BEEDING

The novels of George Moore are little read today, but we can recommend the best known of them, *Esther Waters* (published in 1894) to anyone who enjoys a good traditional tale in a local setting. It's about a devout and rather naive girl who's driven from home by a drunken stepfather at the age of 17 and finds a 'situation' at a house in Upper Beeding. The place is a racing stables, and the naturalness of Moore's descriptions of the gambling fraternity and the low life into which Esther is sucked were regarded as shocking at the end of the last century. Now we can recognize the skill and sensitivity with which the story is told. We shan't spoil your enjoyment by revealing what happens to Esther, and will add only that the novel ends, as it begins, at Upper Beeding.

John Rouse Bloxam was vicar here in the 19th century — brother of Matthew Holbeche Bloxam whose book *Gothic Architecture* was one of the most popular architectural books of its time. The brothers were two of a total of six sons of a former master of Rugby school. All grew to over six feet in height and were noted for their sporting prowess. Their uncle was the painter Sir Thomas Lawrence. [19]

UPPER DICKER

Thomas à Becket's first miracle is said to have been worked in the millrace at Michelham Priory. The story goes that he was returning from the hunt with his friend Gilbert d'Aquila, who lived there, when his horse slipped on the bridge and poor Thomas was thrown into the water. The miracle consisted in his own prayer for survival being answered: the sluices were closed just in time and he climbed out wet but intact.

Owen Emeric Vidal, appointed the first chaplain to the church when it was consecrated around 1840, was in 1852 invited to become bishop of Sierra Leone in West Africa — then known to all as 'the white man's grave'. Fully aware of his likely fate, Vidal unhesitatingly took up the appointment. Within a few years he was dead. A really courageous man in the service of his God, he's remembered by a tablet in the church.

Horatio Bottomley, the larger-than-life orator, MP and fraud, was the squire of the village at the turn of the century, building his mansion, The Dicker, running a racing stud and even developing a race course with a grandstand. (See *Hidden Sussex*). His money was earned through impressing the gullible with grandiose schemes, some of them promoted in his magazine John Bull. He made immense fortunes and lost them several times over, finally being reduced in the Twenties to telling his colourful life story on the stage. Despite his dishonesty (he was sentenced to seven years' penal servitude for his Victory Bonds fraud after the first world war) and his unprepossessing personal appearance, he was immensely popular in the village. When he came out of gaol, the local brass band met him at the railway station he had had especially built to serve The Dicker (now Berwick station) and crowds of wellwishers accompanied him home. Even today it's unwise to speak ill of Horatio Bottomley in the area in which he lived. [22]

UPWALTHAM

It was at Upwaltham that Cardinal Henry Edward Manning (1808-1892) preached his last sermon as an Anglican before joining the Church of Rome. Educated at Harrow and Oxford, following a brilliant academic career, he had taken holy orders in 1832. He went as curate (later rector) of *Woolavington* and with it was curate in charge at the tiny apsidal church of Upwaltham. In 1841 he became archdeacon of Chichester, but was converted to the Roman Catholic church ten years later. In 1865 he became Cardinal Archbishop of Westminster, by which time he was one of the greatest churchmen of his day. [18]

WADHURST

Prize fighting was still much enjoyed in mid-Victorian times. The last such fight took place here in 1863. Three years earlier, Tom Sayers, prominent in the development of pure boxing, had fought an American giant named Heenan, who tried even throttling his opponent. After two hours with no decision, the police arrived, confusion reigned and the battle was forgotten. Tom Sayers was badly injured and a subscription fund was started for him, to which even the Prime Minister contributed. To settle the question of British or American superiority, one Tom King was backed to fight Heenan on a roadside patch near Wadhurst Common. Eventually King's youth and boxing ability turned the scale; but the fight went on for 36 rounds, causing much public indignation and disgust, and in consequence public prize-fighting was made illegal.   [7]

WALBERTON

William Turner, born in Cheshire in 1653, took holy orders and came to Walberton as vicar. Here he wrote one of the most extraordinary books ever conceived. The title begins, 'A Compleat History of the Most Remarkable Providences, Both of Judgment and Mercy, Which have Hapned in this Present Age', and goes on in the same vein for another twenty lines or so. It's usually abbreviated to 'Remarkable Providences'. Among the Sussex villages about which he tells stories are Amberley, Ford and Graffham; but one concerning Shipley is of special interest, as it involves the son of Philip Caryll who was afflicted with scrofula. He addressed himself to King Charles II to be touched for 'the king's evil'. Charles did so, and the lad was shortly cured and shown round the neighbourhood in proof.   [18]

WALDERTON

About 1800 there stood near the bridge here the cottage of "Jack Pitt the gunman". As a youth he worked as a carpenter on the Stansted estate, but probably found being a highwayman more lucrative. Despite the fact that he was a burly six feet one — tall for those times — and made all his attacks at gun-point, nobody recognised him as a highwayman, though they all knew him as an estate worker. He went undetected for years until at the ripe old age of 24 he moved to Portsmouth and turned over a new leaf. He earned an honest livelihood for a couple of years until Fate stepped in. He was brought before Lewes Assizes on a comparatively minor charge, and apparently heard a chance remark which filled him with remorse. He confessed to a series of offences for which he was sentenced to death. He was executed in 1808, aged 27.   [17]

WALDRON

Of all the characters in this book, surely the one most handicapped from birth was poor Fly-Fornication Richardson of Waldron! Let us hope that his Puritan parents permitted the use of a more common name, on weekdays at least.

The original manor was re-named Herindales from the family of Heringaud, who held it from before 1227 to about 1350. In 1227 Sybilla, wife of Nicholas Heringaud, obtained leave of the Prior of Lewes to build a small personal chapel in her court at 'Walderne' — an indication of the power once wielded by monastic establishments.   [22]

WALSTEAD

Soon after the accession of Queen Victoria in 1837 a poor idiot boy of the neighbourhood was often seen wandering, mumbling to himself, into Costell's Wood. After some time he was followed by a neighbour who, to his horror, was led to a decomposed male body lying in the long grass. An open and blood-stained razor lay nearby. Who was the dead man? He was evidently of some standing: his linen was marked T.H. and his boots were of good quality. Nobody in the area had ever seen him, however, and he was never identified. And who (since murder was strongly suspected) had killed him? The idiot boy never told a coherent tale, but nobody thought he could have done the deed. The most plausible theory is that the man had been set upon by footpads and killed for his money.   [12]

WANNOCK

A mystery woman and an indefatigable gardener merit our attention here. After the Belgian baron Jean Cassel bought Filching Manor at the end of the first world war a beautiful woman lived in it. No one knew who she was. When she disappeared in 1929 the house remained empty for 25 years and fell into decay. Ivy smothered the walls, large trees invaded and death-watch beetles made a home there. Enter the gardener hero — a Mr Dodge who, through all those years of neglect, kept nearly three acres of lawn in trim with a 12-inch hand mower! Happy to relate, the manor has now been restored and is even occasionally open to the public.

The most important families living at the Manor in days gone by were the Rochesters and the Markwicks, who'd become related by intermarriage. It belonged to a family called Fennel for a century or so until in 1679 Thomas Markwick acquired it. His brother's nephew Robert Rochester inherited in 1699 and it remained in his family for well over a century. There are three Markwick brasses in Jevington church.   [28]

WARBLETON

Henry Smith was born at Wandsworth in 1548 and became a successful merchant. His wife died long before he did, leaving him childless, so he gave his wealth to the founding of charities, and from about 1620 transferred large areas of land in Sussex to various trustees, some of them of great eminence. He died in January 1627, aged 79, possessed of interests as widely scattered as Alfriston, Hartfield, Rusper, Southwick and Worth. And Warbleton? Here he owned the manor, together with the mansion and manor farm of Iwood. But with a common name, he had to be distinguished from his namesakes. He loved dogs, and was almost always accompanied by one. So he became known, as he still is, as "Dog" Smith.   [23]

WARMINGHURST

A ghost story from 1767. John Butler, a Sussex MP, set off to ride to London from his home at Warminghurst. Early the next morning he appeared before his sister-in-law, but made no reply when she spoke to him. Later Butler's groom returned at a canter, revealing that his master had dropped dead at the precise moment his apparition had been seen.

William Penn the Quaker (see *Hidden Sussex*) lived here for a time.[19]

WARNHAM

The best way to go. Michael Turner, parish clerk here from 1835 until his death 50 years later, was leader of the choir band which played in the old rood loft, and he always wore a white smock frock, red handkerchief, tie and breeches, with an old-fashioned beaver high hat on Sundays. He was a fiddle player who performed at village fairs on the green as well as in church, and he was actually playing the instrument when he died.   [3]

WARNINGCAMP

Things didn't always run smoothly in medieval monastic circles. By the turning off the A27 east of Arundel, and only just inside the hamlet, was a small house of Augustinian canons, called Pynham, founded by Adeliza, Queen of Henry I. A visit of inspection to the place in 1478 unearthed the fact that Prior Gifford was not in the habit of rising during the night for the performance of divine service; that there were then only two resident canons in the house; that they had three men-servants and a boy, of whom only one received pay apart from his food and clothing; and that Thomas Bellyngham, the steward, kept a servant for himself despite the strong objections of the prior.   [18]

WARNINGLID

Lord Tennyson's son wrote a memoir of the great poet describing some of the misadventures attending him and his bride when they set up house here. First a storm blew down part of their bedroom wall, so that wind and rain came in. Then 'they learnt that their dining-room and bedroom had been a Roman Catholic chapel, that a baby was buried somewhere in the house, and later that a gang of thieves and murderers known as 'The Cuckfield Gang' had lived in their very lodge.....that no postman came near the house, that the nearest doctor and butcher (!) lived at Horsham; and that there was not even a carrier who passed anywhere within hail.' No wonder the Tennysons quickly shook the dust of Sussex from their feet. But they did return, years later (see *Aldworth*).

Albert Willard, who died here in 1937, drove the very first motor car in mid Sussex. It was a Benz, and caused a sensation wherever it went.   [11]

WARTLING

In his will dated May 28, 1647 — only a few months before his death — John, Lord Craven, gave certain lands to be sold to raise money. A hundred pounds was to support four poor scholars at Oxford and Cambridge (nearly 200 years later one of these was Thomas Babington Macaulay, later Lord Macaulay the poet and historian), while the remainder was to be used 'in the redemption of English captives in Algiers'.

The memorial board of the radar station here (now at Bexhill Town Hall) includes on its roll the man who was to become famous as Wing Commander Guy Gibson VC of the 'Dambusters'. During the last war 59 enemy aircraft were destroyed with the aid of the radar station.   [23]

WASHINGTON

An entry in the parish register reads: '1631. Mem the 14th of February. Lycence was granted from the Ordinary, under the Lord Bishop's seale, unto Sir John Byne, Knight, and Lady Awdrey his wife, and unto Mr Edmund and Mr John Byne their sonnes, and unto Mrs Elizabeth Byne, wife of the said Edmund, to eat flesh in the time of Lent, at the which time straightly by the King's proclamation, according unto an ancient statute all persons were prohibited from eating of flesh.' The Byne family lived for generations at Rowdell, an estate west of the church; Sir John was knighted by James I on the day before his coronation.

A report in the Sussex Weekly Advertiser in January 1800 reminds us that law enforcement was in hands other than the police in those days. One William Brown of Washington absconded while awaiting trial for sheep stealing and a reward of five guineas was offered for his arrest 'to be paid on his conviction, by the Treasurer of the Washington Society for prosecuting thieves etc'.   [19]

WATERSFIELD

The early 13th century found Bishop Ralph de Nevill having neighbour trouble. Two knights 'claimed to have common' with him — that is, they shared certain rights over his land. They were Sir William Dawtrey and Sir Hugh Sanzaver, and they procured a Writ to take down the fences which the Bishop had erected for the protection of his property. A formal letter written to the Bishop by Simon de Senliz makes it clear that 'they hold nothing of you, and do no service to you to have common with you.'

In 1316 Bishop Langton obtained for this now tiny hamlet a licence for a market and fair, showing that in those times it was a place of some moment — but, after all, the Roman road passed close by, and remains of a Roman bath have been discovered a little way to the north.   [9]

WEST BLATCHINGTON

The Scrase family has been important in Sussex for centuries — certainly by the early 14th century. One Rychard Scras was a personal 'valet' (we should perhaps say equerry) to Henry VIII. His great-grandson was christened Tuppin, his mother's maiden surname, in accordance with then current fashion. By 1616 Tuppin considered himself 'gentry' enough to apply to the College of Arms for a crest. He was granted a design of a falcon standing on the stump of a tree around which a snake curled itself; the curiously-worded grant is reproduced in Vol. 8 of the *Sussex Archaeological Collections*.

His descendant Charles Scrase, who died in 1792, left a large part of his estate to his grandson, Charles Dickins, provided that he assumed the additional surname of Scrase. This was duly done, and even now (in the late 20th century) there are Scrase Dickins of eminence in Sussex.   [20]

WESTBOURNE

References to hermits are scattered throughout Sussex, and through this book. One of the last, and best known, was Simon Cotes of Westbourne, who made a will, still extant, in 1527. He was one of those entrusted with the upkeep of bridges and roads, as we describe under *Southbourne* — indeed, he may even have been the same person, as the old descriptions are ill-defined. He left his house and the chapel he had 'builded' to the Earl of Arundel as a refuge for a professed hermit for ever, to pray for Christian souls.

Henry Garrett Newland, born in London in 1804, became rector of Westbourne in 1829; his family were local lords of the manor. He started to hold a daily service in the church, and to celebrate Holy Communion more often. For so doing he met with bitter opposition from the parishioners, who seem to have felt that it was all right worshipping God so long as you didn't make too much of a habit of it. Newland wrote several theological works, but was keen on fishing and also wrote several popular books on river and forest life.   [30]

WEST BURTON

In *Hidden Sussex* we illustrate the fine early Stuart gateway of Coke's House. The family of Coke (or Cooke) traces back to Thomas Cooke of Heene, now part of Worthing, and became mesne lords of the manor here in the reign of Elizabeth I. Nicholas, the last of five generations of Cookes to live here, died in 1683. [18]

WEST CHILTINGTON

The rector of West Chiltington, John le Susche, fled the area in 1257 after being involved in a fatal brawl with the rector of neighbouring Thakeham, one Martin. The argument seems to have been about the tithes Martin was due to collect. One of le Susche's henchmen shot Martin in the right breast with an arrow and another tried to finish him off with a hatchet. The second man was struck on the head and killed. Martin was tried for murder and acquitted, after which le Susche swiftly disappeared: the hue and cry was raised and 'his chattels are confiscated for flight'. [10]

WEST DEAN, East Sussex

The novels of George Gissing are probably little read today, but in *Thyrza* he describes the village, which he knew well. 'The hamlet consists of a very few houses, all so compactly grouped about the old church that from this distance it seemed as if the hand could cover them. The roofs were overgrown with lichen, yellow on slate, red on tiles... The little group of houses had mellowed with age; their guarded peacefulness was soothing to the eye and the spirit.' [28]

WEST DEAN, West Sussex

Christopher Lewknor was recorder and Member of Parliament for Chichester in the 17th century (West Dean Manor had for some time been the family home) and was a Royalist during the Civil War. He must have been an object of particular hatred to the opposing side because, when Chichester eventually surrendered to the Parliamentary forces in December 1642, the troops plundered and sacked his house with especial venom.

The eccentric Edward James, whom we mention in *Hidden Sussex*, died a few months after its publication and his body was brought back home to West Dean from the remote Mexican jungle where for nearly 40 years he had organised the building of a series of mountainside follies. Said to be the illegitimate son of Edward VII, he inherited 20 million dollars and the West Dean Estate when his nominal father died. He was a poet and a friend of the Surrealist artists Magritte and Dali, and he apparently left Sussex because he was refused permission to build a bronze lake on the estate. His Mexican buildings, none of which was ever finished, have suitably extravagant names: The House on Three Floors Which in Fact will have Five, The House Destined to be a Cinema, and The Summer Palace with Orange Windows, among others. Sporting a white beard on his chin and a parrot on his shoulder, James was popular with the natives. 'They don't treat me as a madman,' he used to say. [17]

WESTFIELD

In about 1100 the manor was held by a man called Wening who gave it by a formal grant to Battle Abbey, and what's remarkable about this is that the manor included a rarity — a pit for carrying out ordeal by water. If the unfortunate victim floated he was adjudged guilty; if he sank he was fished out and declared innocent. **[24]**

WEST GRINSTEAD

Alexander Pope sat under a tree in West Grinstead Park to write that enchanting poem 'The Rape of the Lock' when he was a guest of his friend John Caryll. The Carylls were a great Sussex family and staunch Roman Catholics: there's a priest's hole and a secret chapel at the Clergy House. John Caryll was private secretary to Marie of Modena, James II's wife, for many years, and returned to the family estates at West Grinstead when Queen Anne came to the throne and the religious conflicts appeared to be settled.

William Powlett, who lived in St. Leonard's Forest and died in 1746, was a captain of the Horse Grenadiers in the time of George I. There's a monument to him in West Grinstead church, with a sculpture by the great Michael Rysbrack. Now, a mysterious ghost used to be spoken of as lurking under the name Squire Paulett. The spectre was headless and would leap up behind the riders of horses in the Forest, accompanying them right through to the far side. Several horsemen have left chilly tales of their grisly pillion passenger. **[10]**

WESTHAM

During the 16th century there was a Protestant revolt against stone altars, and nearly all of them were broken up or set into church floors for people to walk on — the latter being the case at Westham. In 1649 John Thatcher, a fervent Roman Catholic at the time when he and his co-religionists were persecuted, left money in trust to 'the Old Brethren' (meaning the Catholic trustees). His three conditions were that the Roman Catholic religion should be restored to England; that Mass should be said for his soul; and that the original altar stone should be re-erected in the church. Will this ever happen? His memorial is in the Priesthawes chapel.
[23]

WESTHAMPNETT

William Gardner, cartographer, was born about 1739, probably in Sussex, and moved to Westhampnett in 1769, a couple of years after beginning in practice as a surveyor. When he married in 1770 at Boxgrove one of the witnesses was Thomas Yeakell, also of Westhampnett. Yeakell and Gardner formed a partnership, doing much of the surveying work for the Duke of Richmond. Yeakell's son, another Thomas, was born in the village in 1762 and was also a surveyor. In 1778 the partners published the first of a series of eight planned maps covering the whole county of Sussex on a scale of two inches to the mile. It was by far the most accurate, detailed and comprehensive survey of the county to that time, and after over two centuries 'Yeakell and Gardner' is still referred to by county topographers and historians — including ourselves.

Among the musicians who played in the church in the days before there were organs, the cornettist here was Charles Norkett, a dwarf of 3ft 4ins who would stand on a stool while playing. He was an enthusiastic cricketer, dying in 1888 at the age of 61 while watching a match at Goodwood.

[17]

WEST HOATHLY

Working conditions have certainly improved since the early 18th century. When Sunak Vinall was bound apprentice to Benjamin Backhall at West Hoathly in 1708 his indenture included the following: 'At Cards Dice or any other unlawful game he shall not play. Ale houses or taverns he shall not haunt. Furthermore, he shall behave himself purely, he shall not contract matrimony....he shall not absent himself by day nor night without the licence or consent of his said Master.' All this simply to learn husbandry work!

J.K. Arundell Esdaile, who lived here for many years, was an author and lecturer, a librarian, a Fellow of the Society of Antiquaries and latterly, Secretary of the British Museum. His father had been distinguished in a different field: he was James Kennedy Esdaile, JP, DL, who lived at Saint Hill, near East Grinstead, and was for some years High Sheriff of Sussex.

One of the most delightful places to visit is the Priest House here. The 13th century building had been owned by Mr J. Godwin King, who kept a personal museum in it and gave the whole to the Sussex Archaeological Society in 1937. [5]

WEST ITCHENOR

During the 1920s the owner and occupier of Itchenor Gate House was A.J. Nixon, a noted conchologist, or expert on seashells. [25]

WESTMESTON

The village's devoted collector of anecdotes is Doris Hall. She tells us that in 1096 a local farmer was strolling along the river bank near Lewes when along the river came a barge laden with stone. In reply to the farmer's query the bargee said his load was 'stone for Wistminster new church'. When the farmer said, 'I be from Wismistern', the bargee replied, 'then it must be for you.' The farmer fetched his cart, loaded the stone and took it home, hiding it under a hayrick. Three years later, when a church was needed, the farmer offered a load of stone to start it. Thus Westmeston church was started with stone originally destined for no less a place than Westminster Abbey.

A story (not from Doris) is told of an old lady from here, who in about 1750 was preparing for a journey to London — her first trip so far from home — to see her married daughter who lived in the capital. A friend asked what sort of place the mother expected to find London. 'Well,' she said, 'I can't exactly tell, but I suppose it must be somethin' like the bustlin' part o' Ditchling.'   [20]

WEST STOKE

The Stoughton family came originally from Surrey, but Adrian lived here for many years, representing Chichester in Parliament in 1597 and again in 1603/4, and being Recorder of Chichester in 1603. Over 31 years his wife Mary presented him with sixteen children, of whom only seven reached maturity. The large, typically Stuart, family monument in the church bears a six-line verse of which the last couplet runs:

> *"Death could not wound him, only clos'd his eye*
> *And made him dye to live that liv'd to dye."*

We haven't discovered Adrian's vocation; could he have been a dyer?
                                                                        [17]

WHATLINGTON

The lord of the manor of Whatlington in 1066 was no less a person than King Harold himself, and later on it was owned in turn by the Pelhams, the Ashburnhams (see *Introduction*) and others. In 1307 John de Watlyngton was made Abbot of Battle.

The manor of Vinehall is also in the parish, and in 1870 M.A. Lower recorded it as then being 'the property and seat of W. Rushton Adamson Esq., by whom it has been re-named Rushton Park.' Lower goes on to give a most interesting snippet, that 'the mansion possesses every appliance of luxury, including gas made on the spot.' Charles Dawson (see *Piltdown*) interested himself in this kind of research, and we think he may have been the discoverer of this gas supply.   [15]

WICK STREET

Just outside the little hamlet lies Claverham Manor which existed before the Conquest. In the late 14th century it belonged to Sir William Fynes (or Fiennes), who had two sons. One was Roger, the builder of Herstmonceux Castle, the other was James, who became the first Lord Say and Sele (see Shakespeare, Henry VI, Part 2, Act 4). Both these eminent natives of Claverham became in later life Treasurers of the King's Household.   **[22]**

WIGGONHOLT

This tiny hamlet is, as we noticed in *Hidden Sussex*, unusually hard to find: it lies down a small lane off the main A283 south of Pulborough. But even such a place as this had, in days gone by, its own little patch of significance. In the reign of Henry III it was owned by Henry Tregoz, who constituted it an independent manor. At this time it extended into no fewer than eight distinct parishes, and in 1492 it was valued at £22. 12s. 7d. Later on the manor was acquired by Sion monastery in Middlesex.   **[10]**

WILLINGDON

Family pride is one thing, but Sir Nicholas Parker's survivors went overboard, as you can see from his tomb in Willingdon churchyard. Born in 1604, he had sided with the Roundheads during the civil war and he was for a time Cromwell's secretary. He wrote books on religion and politics. Here's part of the poem on his tombstone:

> *Then blame not aged Britain's feeble womb,*
> *For in her Parker's birth she did consume*
> *Her utmost strength. The world will scarce be strong*
> *For such another brave conception*   **[28]**

WILMINGTON

Henry Marshall was vicar of Wilmington in the 16th century. He made a long will in 1550 in which, among a string of bequests, he gave to 'my servant William Marshall, if he do lerne an honest occupation or handycraft, x^l (£10), to make him a stock to be delivered when he hath sufficiently lernyd the same: and if he refuse so to doo, I will that he shall have but vi^l. xiij^s. iv^d. (£6 13s.4d.) .... Item, to the said William Marshall one fether bedde, ij paire of sheets, ij blanketts, a bolster, ij pylows, ij pulow bers,' and so on for quite a long inventory, including 'my third brasse pot....a dripping-pan, a lute, my best cote, a rownd pan, a kychyn knyff, and a fire jake.'

The largest of all the People of Hidden Sussex is carved out of the turf on the north face of the Downs here. He was given to the Sussex Archaeological Society by the 9th Duke of Devonshire in 1925. The Long Man was outlined in bricks in 1873, allowed to become overgrown during the second world war so as not to provide a landmark for enemy aircraft and outlined afresh, with white blocks, in 1969. Many are the people who have written about him and theorised about his origins. Despite a good deal of research in the last fifteen years, however, the giant keeps his secret. **[28]**

WINCHELSEA

When Edward I came down to review the Fleet shortly before the new town of Winchelsea was completed (see *Hidden Sussex*) his horse shied during the proceedings and he was precipitated over the wall near the Strand Gate. Fortunately it had been raining heavily and the king survived with no bones broken, though with a thick coating of mud.

Around 1780 two brothers, George and Joseph Weston, lived at The Friars — and lived an amazing double life. They appeared to be virtuous well-to-do citizens and one of them was appointed churchwarden, but their gains came from a series of daring robberies. Eventually they were arrested after a bold attack on the Bristol Mail, and one of them was executed.

John Wesley preached his last open-air service close to the parish church at Winchelsea. His journal for October 7, 1790, reads: 'I went over to that poor skeleton of ancient Winchelsea; it is beautifully situated on the top of a steep hill and was regularly built in broad streets, crossing each other, and encompassing a very large square; in the midst of which was a large church, now in ruins. I stood under a large tree, on the side of it, and called to most of the inhabitants of the town "The kingdom of heaven is at hand; repent and believe the Gospel." It seemed as if all that heard were, for the present, almost persuaded to be Christians.' The scion of that ash tree is growing at the very same place, planted there after the original was struck by lightning.   [24]

WINDMILL HILL

George Luxford of Windmill Hill was a loyal supporter of the future Charles II and *almost* earned himself a knighthood. Apparently Charles planned to reward his staunchest supporters by founding a new order of knights at his Restoration, and Luxford was on the list. Unhappily for him the notion never bore fruit.

J.F. Huxford, in his *Arms of Sussex Families*, confesses himself uncertain as to whether the Luxfords and the Lunsfords were different families or lines of the same one with different spellings. (The coats of arms are almost identical). Sir Thomas Lunsford of Windmill Hill was something of a firebrand, whose story we tell under *East Hoathly*.   [23]

WINEHAM

We've been told a lovely, homely story of a lady who, over seventy years ago, was moving to the village. On moving day she had a dreadful cold, so her family hauled her off to the pub, plied her with drinks, and carried her home and put her to bed. Her daughter, who was sleeping in the same room, was awakened in the early hours by her mother's plaintive call, 'Whatever has happened? I'm in bed and I've still got my gaiters on'![11]

WISBOROUGH GREEN

G.H. Kenyon wrote that indispensable book, *The Glass Industry of the Weald*, in 1967, when he lived at Kirdford. He noted that a number of Huguenot families carried on their traditional craft of glass-making at Wisborough Green between 1567 and 1615. He found many fragments of old glass from the sites he researched, assembled them to make a lancet window which he gave to the church in honour of the exiled Frenchmen.

In his book he tells of a quarrel in 1606 between Albert Hensey, a trained glassmaker, and Thomas Jackson, who owned a glass-house, or workshop. On February 7, while Hensey was at church, Jackson 'riotously assembled' a gang of a dozen or so and set upon Hensey's workmen in an attempt to take over his premises. When that failed, they laid siege to it, even beating the wives and daughters of several of the men who tried to take food to them. As so often, the outcome of the battle is not recorded. [**9**]

WISTON

Heinrich ('Heinz') Koeppler, born in Prussia in 1912, came to England in 1933 as a post-graduate student at Oxford. During the 1939-1945 War he served the British Government in the Political Warfare Executive. In 1943 Sir Winston Churchill was seeking creative ideas about post-war Germany, and Koeppler suggested setting up a centre in England where Germans with little experience of democracy could meet British and other people and discuss common ideas. The vision became reality on January 12, 1946, when the first Conference assembled at Wilton Park (Bucks.). From 1950 on, Conferences were held in Sussex at Wiston House, which became known also as Wilton Park. Since 1957 the conferences have been open to all the OECD countries. Sir Heinz, as he became, acted as Warden of Wilton Park from 1946 to 1977. He died on April 1, 1979, leaving a substantial portion of his large estate to Wilton Park. But he drew up the bequest in his own informal words, and a legal action, which reached the Court of Appeal in 1985, was needed to establish whether his gift was legally valid or not.

Sir Thomas Sherley, of a family settled in Sussex since 1450, in 1605 devised an ingenious scheme for enabling the purchase of the honour of a 'baronetcy' — it brought much needed funds into James I's depleted coffers. Sir Thomas died in 1612, leaving three sons, Thomas, Anthony and Robert, all of whom were among the blades of their days. Thomas became an MP, engaged in speculative and disastrous sea voyages to Constantinople and Venice, and got himself imprisoned in the Tower. Anthony became a barrister but preferred a life of adventure in Persia, Morocco, Russia and Spain, which did him no good as he died a pauper. Robert stayed in Persia for several years, before becoming a roving ambassador for the king around the Mediterranean. He returned to Persia in 1623 and died there. [**19**]

WITHDEAN

William Roe, between 1775 and 1809, kept what he called 'private memorandums' in four manuscript books, which were privately printed by Charles Thomas-Stanford in 1928, and full of interest they are.

Roe, born in Glamorgan in 1748, married a Yapton girl in 1775, at St. George's Hanover Square. He held a series of important posts in the Civil Service of the day, culminating in membership of the Board for African Claims, which oversaw and eventually abolished the slave trade. He bought Withdean Manor in 1794 for £13,000. He records in proud detail the new tree plantations he makes, and one can imagine his dismay in 1800 when he received a letter 'informing me that on Sunday the 9th there had been the highest wind at Withdean known in the memory of man and that 14 or 15 of my oldest Elms were blown down by the Storm and some blown asunder...In general the mischief took effect in bottoms or Gullies between the Hills.' [20]

WITHYHAM

At Buckhurst in this parish was born Thomas Sackville, earliest of the long line of the family to achieve undying renown. He sat in Parliament in the reign of Elizabeth I, and after a long career was in 1599 made Lord High Treasurer of England. The Queen had created him Lord Buckhurst in 1567, and her successor, King James I, made him Earl of Dorset in 1604. He died in 1608, but his writings are still studied today. In 1563 he wrote part of a long narrative poem entitled *A Mirrour for Magistrates*, and collaborated with Thomas Norton to write *Gorboduc*, the earliest surviving English tragic play with any pretension to merit. [29]

WITTERINGS, The

The name of Oliver Whitby ought to be better known than it is. He was born in 1664, the son of another Oliver Whitby who was an Archdeacon of Chichester. Our Oliver lived in Harting, and then in London and Chichester, where he died in 1702, aged only 38. He left in his will his lands at West Wittering to establish a school at which the boys should wear blue gowns. The Trustees bought a house in West Street, Chichester, where the original Bluecoat School was opened in 1712. It remained there until 1951, when the pupils were transferred to Christ's Hospital, Horsham. A wooden figure of an 'Oliver Whitby' Bluecoat boy is in Chichester Museum.

The Tipteers were six boys or men dressed in fantastic costume, some carrying wooden swords. They enacted a short play, generally around Christmastime, whose words were handed down by oral tradition. The characters were King George, a noble Captain, whom he wounds, a Knight of Turkey, Old Father Christmas and a Doctor, besides a number of nondescript men. Its age is unknown, but from the words it must go back for centuries. A version of it was printed in Vol. 44 of the *Sussex Archaelogical Collections*.[25]

WIVELSFIELD

Selina Shirley, later the Countess of Huntingdon, was a remarkable if perhaps a rather daunting woman. Born in 1707, she married the ninth Earl of Huntingdon in 1728 and for more than 20 years lived mostly in his country house in Leicestershire, where his sister was also a fixture. The sister converted Selina to the cause of evangelical Methodism, with such success that after her husband's death she had her own chaplain specifically charged with the duty of promulgating her views to the world. She came to Sussex around 1750 and for some time Great Ote Hall, Wivelsfield, was her home: one of the rooms was even supplied with a pulpit from which the chaplain would preach. As she was wealthy she was able to build and endow a number of churches in Sussex (together forming the Countess of Huntingdon's Connection), including the one here with her name on it and a big church in Brighton which was demolished only in the 1970s.

Two days before Christmas 1899 a railway disaster here, in dense fog, caused the death of at least six people, with some twenty seriously injured. The driver of one of the trains, the Continental from Newhaven, recounted the tragedy in verse which wouldn't have shamed William McGonagall:

We went our way well up to time, when a signal came in sight,
  When bang, bang, went the signals and the fogman showed a light.
I very soon applied the brakes, the train was steadied down
  To walking pace, as the distant signal was not down.
Wivelsfield soon we reached, five minutes there we waited,
  Where the signal stood at danger, of this we were acquainted
By the fogman, who stood watching to tell us when 'twas 'right',
  The signal fell, and off we started, wishing him 'good-night'.
I scarcely had the steam put on, when I felt a jerk and strain,
  Which plainly told a serious thing had happened to our train.
The engine then I quickly stopped and saw an awful sight,
  As back along the track I went on that memorable night;
I heard the screams that rent the air, it gave me such a shock,
  Then off I ran and told a man the down line he must block,
Because an engine there was laid far over on her side,
  Wrecked carriages lying all about on the line from side to side....

In *Hidden Sussex* we mentioned the remains of an old gate post on the B2112. A correspondent tells us he remembers there being a five-barred gate to prevent cattle straying from Ditchling Common. He adds: 'There was another gate on the edge of the common, on the road from the B2112 to Wivelsfield Station. The latter was manned, if I can call it that, by a retarded boy who suffered from fits. People passing, especially in horse-drawn vehicles, threw him coppers so that they were saved from dismounting and opening and closing the gate. He had a fit one day and fell face down in quite a small puddle and was drowned.' [11]

WOODMANCOTE

The 'Marian Persecutions' of 1556, when Protestants were hounded by reason of the Catholic sympathies of Queen Mary Tudor, are remembered in Sussex to this day — and not without cause. Many devout Protestants were martyred by being burned alive. Among those whose names are on record are Thomas Harland and John Oswald who came from the tiny hamlet of Woomancote. Its smallness suggests that it may have been what Authority would have called 'a hotbed of heresy'. [20]

WOOLAVINGTON

Emily Sargent and her sister Caroline, daughters of the rector of Woolavington, both married churchmen — and churchmen who rose to great distinction. Caroline's husband, Henry Manning, was the curate and later rector of Woolavington, finishing his career as the Roman Catholic Cardinal Archbishop of Westminster (we tell his story under *Upwaltham*). Emily married Samuel Wilberforce, who was to become Bishop of Oxford and Winchester and just missed promotion to Archbishop of Canterbury. Crosses in the churchyard mark the graves of the bishop, Emily and Caroline (who died after only four years of marriage) while inside the church you can see the bishop's beautifully carved crozier. The sisters were nieces of the Captain Sargent whose story we narrate under *Graffham*. [9]

WOOLBEDING

More of those tantalising glimpses into the past which cry out for elucidation! In 1338 Eve, widow of William Paynel, held the manor of 'Wolbeding': she had by then remarried. Still alive in 1354, she is known to have held the manor 'by service of coming before the King with the infantry to the bridge of Shetebrugge and from there carrying a standard to Wolwardebrugge.' Then in the time of Henry VIII Edmund Gray held the tenure of the manor of Woolbeding 'by service of carrying before the lord King a bow without a string and bolt without feathers whenever the King comes in those parts, namely when he is going to cross to Hampshire from the bridge called Wolversbridge, near Midhurst to the bridge of Sheet in Hampshire'. Clearly empty ceremonial isn't a modern invention.

'A bolt (or bird-bolt)' writes J. F. Huxford, 'was a short blunt arrow used for shooting birds. Heraldically they are shown with the ends either flat, round or forked. Bows without strings and bolts without feathers seem rather useless articles chosen to carry before the monarch. Perhaps it was felt they offered no threat to the person of the king's majesty.' [8]

WORTH

Leonard Gale was born of humble parents in 1610, but his is one of the county's great success stories. He saved his money a penny at a time as a young lad, and in his early twenties he came to Sussex from his native Sevenoaks, took over St Leonard's Forge and started up as an ironmaster. He spent 15 years in partnership with Walter Burrell of Knepp Castle and then went his own way, buying Tinsloe Forge. At the age of 66 he was worth at least £16,000 — no small sum in the days of Charles II — and he died in 1690. He left most of his estate to his son Leonard, who was called to the Bar. In 1698 he bought the large Crabbet estate for £8,000; in 1710 he was elected MP for East Grinstead; and by 1724 he was worth, according to his own calculations, upwards of £40,000. He died in 1750 and is buried in Worth church.

Robert Whitehead (1823-1905), inventor of the first successful torpedo, lived at Paddockhurst (now Worth Abbey). Wilfred Scawen Blunt, poet, diplomat and aficionado of Arab racehorses, lived at Crabbet Park where his daughter, the Baroness Wentworth (great granddaughter of the poet Byron) bred horses.   [4]

YAPTON

We mention wife-selling elsewhere, but a peculiar bargain was struck at the local pub, the Shoulder of Mutton and Cucumbers, at the turn of the century. The local rat-catcher, a man named White, lodged at the pub, and he took a fancy to the wife of a thatcher called Marley. The two came to a bargain at the bar: the rat-catcher took Mrs Marley, the children and the furniture while the thatcher settled for 7s.6d. and a quart of beer.

As we breathe our last on these pages let's salute Bognor's voluntary fire brigade, whose members were dragged from local hostelries one night early this century to attend a fire at Yapton. They harnessed the horses and drove hell-for-leather to the scene — too fast, indeed, for the old grey mare at the front which had no sooner come to a halt than she collapsed and died. 'Well, I'm danged,' declared her owner to the sympathetic crowd, 'I've never known her do that before!'   [18]

Books for the record . . .

All the books listed in *Hidden Sussex* have helped us again, and we are glad to acknowledge our debt. Many other books which we've consulted and sometimes been able to acquire are mentioned in the text, because they relate to specific villages or areas. The best new book since *Hidden Sussex* appeared eighteen months ago has been 'The West Sussex Village Book' by Tony Wales (Countryside Books) — we believe an East Sussex counterpart is under way. Tony Wales mentions fewer places than we have done, but he gives each one more coverage.

The list of recent publications has been too large for us to read them all, but 'Smuggling in Kent and Sussex 1700 to 1840' by Mary Waugh (also Countryside Books) is a full-scale treatment of her subject. Messrs. Phillimores Ltd. of Chichester are issuing a large range of well-illustrated local books, preserving much history which was in danger of being lost. We've also had much help from their 'Sussex Bells and Belfries' (G. P. Elphick), and 'Arms of Sussex Families' (J. F. Huxford).

Among older books, we must single out the two volumes of 'Glimpses of our Sussex Ancestors' (Charles Fleet — 1882); 'Sussex Church Music in the Past' (K. H. MacDermott — 1922); 'Downland Pathways' (1924) and 'Waters of Arun' (1930), both by A. H. Allcroft; 'Mid-Sussex through the Ages' (A. H. Gregory, 1938); and the various works by Viscountess Wolseley. For more general reading, we have gleaned help from 'A Field Guide to the English Country Parson' (T. Hinde — Heinemann); Cobbett's 'Rural Rides'; most of the medieval chronicles; and several volumes in Methuen's 'Antiquary's Books' series, published earlier this century.

We must not omit the annual volumes of the Sussex Archaeological Society. The earlier issues in particular have been invaluable, as the articles on families and individuals are detailed and authoritative. The Victoria County History of Sussex, revived after many years, has put us in its debt with a comprehensive index to the first six volumes published.

We have tried to identify our sources, but if inadvertently we have left any unnamed, we apologise and trust we may be forgiven.

Lastly, we must thank the Brighton antiquarian booksellers Messrs. Holleyman & Treacher Ltd. for allowing us the run of their shelves and for finding much rare material.

Toll house, Kingston (East Sussex)

INDEX OF NAMES

164

SUBJECT INDEX (selective)

NOTE: To index every subject touched on in this book would mean having an index almost as large as the book. We have therefore selected a few headings which we think will be useful. Our work can always be supplemented on a separate sheet.